To

Dad

From

Sharon Baptist Church

Date

June 15, 2008

W OMACK
Z Cor 5
16-17

99
QUESTIONS
GOD'S ANSWERS
for Dads

The quoted ideas expressed in this book (but not Scripture verses) are not, in all cases, exact quotations, as some have been edited for clarity and brevity. In all cases, the author has attempted to maintain the speaker's original intent. In some cases, quoted material for this book was obtained from secondary sources, primarily print media. While every effort was made to ensure the accuracy of these sources, the accuracy cannot be guaranteed. For additions, deletions, corrections, or clarifications in future editions of this text, please write Freeman-Smith, LLC.

Scripture quotations are taken from:

The Holy Bible, King James Version (KJV)

The Holy Bible, New International Version (NIV) Copyright © 1973, 1978, 1984, by International Bible Society. Used by permission of Zondervan Publishing House. All rights reserved.

The Holy Bible, New King James Version (NKJV) Copyright © 1982 by Thomas Nelson, Inc. Used by permission.

Holy Bible, New Living Translation, (NLT) copyright © 1996. Used by permission of Tyndale House Publishers, Inc., Wheaton, Illinois 60189. All rights reserved.

The Message (MSG)- This edition issued by contractual arrangement with NavPress, a division of The Navigators, U.S.A. Originally published by NavPress in English as THE MESSAGE: The Bible in Contemporary Language copyright 2002-2003 by Eugene Peterson. All rights reserved.

New Century Version®. (NCV) Copyright © 1987, 1988, 1991 by Word Publishing, a division of Thomas Nelson, Inc. All rights reserved. Used by permission.

The New American Standard Bible®, (NASB) Copyright © 1960, 1962, 1963, 1968, 1971, 1972, 1973, 1975, 1977, 1995 by The Lockman Foundation. Used by permission.

The Holman Christian Standard Bible™ (HOLMAN CSB) Copyright © 1999, 2000, 2001 by Holman Bible Publishers. Used by permission.

Cover Design Kim Russell / Wahoo Designs

Page Layout by Bart Dawson

ISBN 978-1-58334-117-9

Printed in the United States of America

99
QUESTIONS
GOD'S ANSWERS
for Dads

❓ INDEX OF TOPICS

Introduction

Because you're reading this book, you probably answer to the name "Dad," "Daddy," "Father," or some variation thereof—if so, congratulations. As a loving father you have been blessed by your children and by God.

As a thoughtful man living in a challenging world, you probably have questions, lots of questions. And if you've got questions, God has answers. Your challenge, of course, is to discover those answers (from God's Holy Word) and then apply them to the challenges of everyday living. And this book can help.

This text contains 99 questions that Christian dads are likely to ask, along with answers based upon truths contained in God's ultimate guidebook: the Holy Bible.

Fatherhood is both a priceless gift from God and an unrelenting responsibility. This text is intended to remind you that, when it comes to the tough job of being a responsible parent, you and God, working together, are destined to do great things for your kids and for the world.

? QUESTION 1

As a busy dad, I feel overwhelmed sometimes. What can I do?

THE QUICK ANSWER

One way to battle the rigors of fatherhood is to slow down long enough to take stock of your blessings, starting with your family.

You Are Blessed

The Lord bless you and keep you; The Lord make His face shine upon you, And be gracious to you.
Numbers 6:24-25 NKJV

Because you are a father, you have been specially blessed by God. God has given you blessings that are too numerous to count. Your blessings include life, family, freedom, friends, talents, and possessions, for starters. But, your greatest blessing—a gift that is yours for the asking—is God's gift of salvation through Christ Jesus.

The gifts you receive from God are multiplied when you share them with others. Today, give thanks to God for your blessings and demonstrate your gratitude by sharing those blessings with your family and with the world.

Think of the blessings we so easily take for granted: Life itself; preservation from danger; every bit of health we enjoy; every hour of liberty; the ability to see, to hear, to speak, to think, and to imagine all this comes from the hand of God.

Billy Graham

Blessings can either humble us and draw us closer to God or allow us to become full of pride and self-sufficiency.

Jim Cymbala

God's kindness is not like the sunset—brilliant in its intensity, but dying every second. God's generosity keeps coming and coming and coming.

Bill Hybels

God is more anxious to bestow His blessings on us than we are to receive them.

St. Augustine

A PRAYER FOR DADS

Today, Lord, I count my many blessings, beginning with my family. You have cared for me, Lord, and I will give thanks and praise You always. Today, let me share Your gifts with others, just as You first shared them with me. Amen

? QUESTION 2

What does the Bible say about putting God first in my life?

THE QUICK ANSWER

God's Word is clear: If you put Him first in every aspect of your life, you'll be blessed. But if you relegate God to a position of lesser importance, you'll distance yourself from His blessings.

Who's First?

The thing you should want most is God's kingdom
and doing what God wants. Then all these other things
you need will be given to you.
Matthew 6:33 NCV

As you think about the nature of your relationship with God, remember this: you will always have some type of relationship with Him—it is inevitable that your life must be lived in relationship to God. The question is not if you will have a relationship with Him; the burning question is whether or not that relationship will be one that seeks to honor Him.

Are you willing to place God first in your life? And, are you willing to welcome God's Son into your heart? Unless you can honestly answer these questions with a resounding yes, then your relationship with God isn't what it could be or should be. Thankfully, God is always available, He's always ready to forgive, and He's waiting to hear from you now. The rest, of course, is up to you.

God is able to do anything He pleases with one ordinary person fully consecrated to Him.

Henry Blackaby and Claude King

God calls us to be committed to Him, to be committed to making a difference, and to be committed to reconciliation.

Bill Hybels

God deserves first place in your life . . . and you deserve the experience of putting Him there.

Jim Gallery

A PRAYER FOR DADS

Dear Lord, today I will honor You with my thoughts, my actions, and my prayers. I will seek to please You, and I will strive to serve You. Your blessings are as limitless as Your love. And because I have been so richly blessed, I will worship You, Father, with thanksgiving in my heart and praise on my lips, this day and forever. Amen

QUESTION 3

It's a noisy world. What does the Bible say about finding time for quiet reflection?

THE QUICK ANSWER

Time and again, God's Word encourages believers to quiet themselves and spend silent moments with the Father. So begin each day with a few minutes of quiet time to organize your thoughts and praise your Creator.

Time for Silence

Be silent before the Lord and wait expectantly for Him.
Psalm 37:7 Holman CSB

Do you take time each day for an extended period of silence? And during those precious moments, do you sincerely open your heart to your Creator? If so, you are wise and you are blessed.

The world can be a noisy place, a place filled to the brim with distractions, interruptions, and frustrations. And if you're not careful, the struggles and stresses of everyday living can rob you of the peace that should rightfully be yours because of your personal relationship with Christ. So take time each day to quietly commune with your Savior. When you do, those moments of silence will enable you to participate more fully in the only source of peace that endures: God's peace.

If the pace and the push, the noise and the crowds are getting to you, it's time to stop the nonsense and find a place of solace to refresh your spirit.

Charles Swindoll

Silence is as fit a garment for devotion as any other language.

C. H. Spurgeon

Growth takes place in quietness, in hidden ways, in silence and solitude. The process is not accessible to observation.

Eugene Peterson

A PRAYER FOR DADS

Dear Lord, in the quiet moments of this day, I will turn my thoughts and prayers to You. In silence I will sense Your presence, and I will seek Your will for my life, knowing that when I accept Your peace, I will be blessed today and throughout eternity. Amen

QUESTION 4

Sometimes, when I'm supposed to be having fun, I feel guilty. What does the Bible say about fun?

THE QUICK ANSWER

Today and every day, God wants you to rejoice. In fact, He teaches us that every day is a cause for celebration: So don't feel guilty about having good, clean fun. As long as you're following in the footsteps of His Son, God approves.

Time for Fun

So I recommend having fun, because there is nothing better for people to do in this world than to eat, drink, and enjoy life. That way they will experience some happiness along with all the hard work God gives them.

Ecclesiastes 8:15 NLT

Are you a man who takes time each day to really enjoy life? Hopefully so. After all, you are the recipient of a precious gift—the gift of life. And because God has seen fit to give you this gift, it is incumbent upon you to use it and to enjoy it. But sometimes, amid the inevitable pressures of everyday living, really enjoying life may seem almost impossible. It is not.

For most of us, fun is as much a function of attitude as it is a function of environment. So whether you're standing victorious atop one of life's mountains or trudging through one of life's valleys, enjoy yourself. You deserve to have fun today, and God wants you to have fun today . . . so what on earth are you waiting for?

_____

If we don't hunger and thirst after righteousness, we'll become anemic and feel miserable in our Christian experience.

Franklin Graham

True happiness and contentment cannot come from the things of this world. The blessedness of true joy is a free gift that comes only from our Lord and Savior, Jesus Christ.

Dennis Swanberg

The happiest people in the world are not those who have no problems, but the people who have learned to live with those things that are less than perfect.

James Dobson

A PRAYER FOR DADS

Dear Lord, You are my strength and my joy. I will rejoice in the day that You have made, and I will give thanks for the countless blessings that You have given me. Let me be a joyful Christian, Father, as I share the Good News of Your Son, and let me praise You for all the marvelous things You have done. Amen

What does the Bible have to say about happiness?

THE QUICK ANSWER

Jesus intends for our joy to be complete (John 15:11). And He came to earth so that we might experience His abundance (John 10:10). So, if we're wise, we'll open our hearts to Christ and celebrate His gifts today, tomorrow, and forever.

A Happy Christian

Happy are the people whose strength is in You,
whose hearts are set on pilgrimage.
Psalm 84:5 Holman CSB

Happiness depends less upon our circumstances than upon our thoughts. When we turn our thoughts to God, to His gifts, and to His glorious creation, we experience the joy that God intends for His children. But, when we focus on the negative aspects of life, we suffer needlessly.

Do you sincerely want to be a happy Christian? Then set your mind and your heart upon God's love and His grace. The fullness of life in Christ is available to all who seek it and claim it. Count yourself among that number. Seek first the salvation that is available through a personal relationship with Jesus

Christ, and then claim the joy, the peace, and the spiritual abundance that the Shepherd offers His sheep.

There is no correlation between wealth and happiness.

Larry Burkett

Our thoughts, not our circumstances, determine our happiness.

John Maxwell

Whoever possesses God is happy.

St. Augustine

God has charged Himself with full responsibility for our eternal happiness and stands ready to take over the management of our lives the moment we turn in faith to Him.

A. W. Tozer

A PRAYER FOR DADS

Dear Lord, You are my strength and my joy. I will rejoice in the day that You have made, and I will give thanks for the countless blessings that You have given me. Let me be a joyful Christian, Father, as I share Your Good News with friends, with family, and with the world. Amen

QUESTION 6

Tough times are inevitable. What should I do when I encounter adversity?

THE QUICK ANSWER

First: Trust God. Next, pray early and often. Then, face your challenges head-on. And finally, remember that there's nothing you'll face today that you and God, working together, can't handle.

Tackling Tough Times

God is our refuge and strength, always ready to help in times of trouble. So we will not fear, even if earthquakes come and mountains crumble to the sea.
Psalm 46:1-2 NLT

Are you a dad who has endured tough times? If so, welcome to the club! From time to time, all of us face adversity, discouragement, or disappointment. When we do, God stands ready to protect us. Psalm 147 promises, "He heals the brokenhearted, and binds their wounds" (v. 3, NIV). When we are troubled, we must call upon God, and then, in His own time and according to His own plan, He will heal us.

Life is often challenging, but as Christians, we must not be afraid. God loves us, and He will protect us. In times of hardship, He will comfort us; in times of sorrow, He will dry our tears. When we are troubled or weak or sorrowful, God is always with us. We must build our lives on the rock that cannot be shaken . . . we must trust in God. Always.

Your greatest ministry will likely come out of your greatest hurt.

Rick Warren

Jesus does not say, "There is no storm." He says, "I am here, do not toss, but trust."

Vance Havner

Throughout history, when God's people found themselves facing impossible odds, they reminded themselves of God's limitless power.

Bill Hybels

A PRAYER FOR DADS

Heavenly Father, You are my strength and my refuge. As I journey through this day, I know that I may encounter disappointments and losses. When I am troubled, let me turn to You. Keep me steady, Lord, and renew a right spirit inside of me this day and forever. Amen

QUESTION 7

What does the Bible have to say about my life?

THE QUICK ANSWER

Every human life (including yours) is a precious gift from God. So celebrate! And while you're at it, praise God for His blessings, and follow in the footsteps of His Son. When you do these things, you'll experience the peace and abundance that only God can give.

A Life to Be Treasured

For whoever finds me finds life and receives favor from the LORD.
Proverbs 8:35 NIV

Life can be tough sometimes, but it's also wonderful—and it's a glorious gift from God. How will you use that gift? Will you treat this day as a precious treasure from your Heavenly Father, or will you take the next 24 hours for granted? The answer should be obvious: Every day, including this one, comes gift-wrapped from God—your job is to unwrap that gift, to use it wisely, and to give thanks to the Giver.

Instead of sleepwalking through life, you and your family members must wake up and live in the precious present. Each waking moment holds the potential to celebrate, to serve, to share, or to love. Because you are a person with incalculable potential, each moment has incalculable value. Your challenge is to experience each day to the fullest as you seek to live in accordance with God's plan for your life. When you do, you'll experience His abundance and His peace.

Are you willing to treat this day (and every one hereafter) as a special gift to be savored and celebrated? You should—and if you seek to Live with a capital L, you most certainly will.

You've heard the saying, "Life is what you make it." That means we have a choice. We can choose to have a life full of frustration and fear, but we can just as easily choose one of joy and contentment.

Dennis Swanberg

People, places, and things were never meant to give us life. God alone is the author of a fulfilling life.

Gary Smalley & John Trent

A PRAYER FOR DADS

Dear Lord, You have created this glorious universe, and You have created me. Let me live my life to the fullest, and let me use my life for Your glory, today and every day. Amen

? QUESTION 8

I try to do my best, but sometimes, despite my best efforts, I make big mistakes. What does the Bible say about that?

THE QUICK ANSWER

Time and again, the Bible preaches the power of perseverance. Setbacks, disappointments, and failures are inevitable—your response to them is optional. If you don't give up, you can turn your stumbling blocks into stepping stones . . . and you should.

Beyond Failure

Success, success to you, and success to those who help you,
for your God will help you . . . .
1 Chronicles 12:18 NIV

The occasional disappointments and failures of life are inevitable. Such setbacks are simply the price that we must occasionally pay for our willingness to take risks as we follow our dreams. But even when we encounter bitter disappointments, we must never lose faith.

As parents, we are far from perfect. And, without question, our children are imperfect as well. When we make mistakes, we must correct them and learn from them. And, when our children make mistakes, we must help them do likewise.

No matter how badly we have failed, we can always get up and begin again. Our God is the God of new beginnings.

Warren Wiersbe

Success or failure can be pretty well predicted by the degree to which the heart is fully in it.

John Eldredge

If you learn from a defeat, you have not really lost.

Zig Ziglar

Our problem isn't that we've failed. Our problem is that we haven't failed enough. We haven't been brought low enough to learn what God wants us to learn.

Charles Swindoll

A PRAYER FOR DADS

Dear Lord, when I encounter failures and disappointments, keep me mindful that You are in control. Let me persevere—even if my soul is troubled—and let me follow Your Son, Jesus Christ, this day and forever. Amen

?QUESTION 9

Sometimes it's hard to be a patient parent. What advice can I find in God's Word?

THE QUICK ANSWER

God's Word teaches that patience is better than strength (Proverbs 16:32). So wise parents learn to control anger before anger controls them.

The Power of Patience

Be gentle to everyone, able to teach, and patient.
2 Timothy 2:23 Holman CSB

The rigors of parenting can test the patience of the most even-tempered dads. From time to time, even the most mannerly children may do things that worry us or confuse us or anger us. Why? Because they are children and because they are human. As loving parents, we must be patient with our children's shortcomings (just as they, too, must be patient with ours).

Sometimes, patience is the price we pay for being responsible fathers, and that's as it should be. After all, think how patient our Heavenly Father has been with us.

You can't step in front of God and not get in trouble. When He says, "Go three steps," don't go four.

Charles Stanley

In all negotiations of difficulties, a man may not look to sow and reap at once. He must prepare his business and so ripen it by degrees.

Francis Bacon

As we wait on God, He helps us use the winds of adversity to soar above our problems. As the Bible says, "Those who wait on the LORD . . . shall mount up with wings like eagles."

Billy Graham

Teach us, O Lord, the disciplines of patience, for to wait is often harder than to work.

Peter Marshall

A PRAYER FOR DADS

Heavenly Father, let me wait quietly for You. Let me live according to Your plan and according to Your timetable. When I am hurried, slow me down. When I become impatient with others, give me empathy. Today, I want to be a patient Christian, Dear Lord, as I trust in You and in Your master plan. Amen

What does the Bible say about the need to serve others?

THE QUICK ANSWER

Whether you realize it or not, God has called you to a life of service. Your job is to find a place to serve and get busy.

A Willingness to Serve

You address me as "Teacher" and "Master," and rightly so.
That is what I am. So if I, the Master and Teacher,
washed your feet, you must now wash each other's feet.
I've laid down a pattern for you. What I've done, you do.
John 13:15 MSG

Jesus teaches that the most esteemed men and women are not the leaders of society or the captains of industry. To the contrary, Jesus teaches that the greatest among us are those who choose to minister and to serve.

Today, you may feel the temptation to build yourself up in the eyes of your neighbors. Resist that temptation. Instead, serve your neighbors quietly and without fanfare. Find a need and fill it . . . humbly. Lend a helping hand and share a word of kindness . . . anonymously.

Today, take the time to minister to those in need. Then, when you have done your best to serve your neighbors and to serve your God, you can rest comfortably knowing that in the eyes of God, you have achieved greatness. And God's eyes, after all, are the only ones that really count.

In Jesus, the service of God and the service of the least of the brethren were one.

Dietrich Bonhoeffer

God does not do anything with us, only through us.

Oswald Chambers

Make it a rule, and pray to God to help you to keep it, never, if possible, to lie down at night without being able to say: "I have made one human being at least a little wiser, or a little happier, or at least a little better this day."

Charles Kingsley

A PRAYER FOR DADS

Dear Lord, when Jesus humbled Himself and became a servant, He also became an example for me. Make me a faithful steward of my gifts, and let me be a humble servant to my loved ones, to my friends, and to those in need. Amen

? QUESTION 11

What does the Bible say about discipline?

THE QUICK ANSWER

Time and again, the Bible praises discipline. A disciplined lifestyle gives you more control: The more disciplined you become, the more you can take control over your life (which, by the way, is far better than letting your life take control over you).

Discipline Now

But I discipline my body and bring it into subjection, lest,
when I have preached to others, I myself should become disqualified.
1 Corinthians 9:27 NKJV

Are you a self-disciplined dad? If so, congratulations . . . if not, God wants to have a little talk with you.

You live in a world in which leisure is glorified and indifference is often glamorized. But God has other plans. He did not create you to be ordinary; He created you for far greater things.

Life's greatest rewards aren't likely to fall into your lap. To the contrary, your greatest accomplishments will probably require lots of work, which is perfectly fine with God. After all,

He knows that you're up to the task, and He has big plans for you. God will do His part to fulfill those plans, and the rest, of course, is up to you.

Now, are you steadfast in your determination to be a self-disciplined man? If so, congratulations . . . if not, reread this little essay—and keep reading it—until God's message finally sinks in.

If one examines the secret behind a championship football team, a magnificent orchestra, or a successful business, the principal ingredient is invariably discipline.

James Dobson

Personal humility is a spiritual discipline and the hallmark of the service of Jesus.

Franklin Graham

Work is doing it. Discipline is doing it every day. Diligence is doing it well every day.

Dave Ramsey

A PRAYER FOR DADS

Lord, make me a man of discipline and righteousness. Let me teach others by the faithfulness of my conduct, and let me follow Your will and Your Word, today and every day. Amen

So many people around me seem to need encouragement. What should I do?

THE QUICK ANSWER

Do you want to be successful and go far in life? Encourage others to do the same. You can't lift other people up without lifting yourself up, too. And remember the words of Oswald Chambers: "God grant that we may not hinder those who are battling their way slowly into the light."

The Gift of Encouragement

Let's see how inventive we can be in encouraging love and helping out, not avoiding worshipping together as some do but spurring each other on.
Hebrews 10:24-25 MSG

Every member of your family needs a regular supply of encouraging words and pats on the back. And you need the rewards that God gives to those enthusiastic dads who are a continual source of encouragement to their wives and children.

In his letter to the Ephesians, Paul writes, "Do not let any unwholesome talk come out of your mouths, but only what is helpful for building others up according to their needs, that it may benefit those who listen" (4:29 NIV). This passage reminds us that, as Christians, we are instructed to choose our words carefully so as to build others up through wholesome, honest encouragement. How can we build others up? By celebrating their victories and their accomplishments. As the old saying goes, "When someone does something good, applaud—you'll make two people happy."

Today, look for the good in others—starting with your family. And then, celebrate the good that you find. When you do, you'll be a powerful force of encouragement in the world . . . and a worthy servant to your God.

We urgently need people who encourage and inspire us to move toward God and away from the world's enticing pleasures.

Jim Cymbala

A PRAYER FOR DADS

Dear Lord, make me a man who is quick to celebrate the accomplishments of others. Make me a source of genuine, lasting encouragement to my family and friends. And let my words and deeds be worthy of Your Son, the One who gives me strength and salvation, this day and for all eternity. Amen

Life is an exercise in making choices. How does God want me to choose?

THE QUICK ANSWER

God wants you to study His Word, to follow His Son, and to make choices accordingly.

Choices

I am offering you life or death, blessings or curses.
Now, choose life! . . . To choose life is to love the Lord your God,
obey him, and stay close to him.
Deuteronomy 30:19-20 NCV

Life is a series of decisions and choices. Each day, we make countless decisions that can bring us closer to God...or not. When we live according to God's commandments, we earn for ourselves the abundance and peace that He intends for our lives. But, when we turn our backs upon God by disobeying Him, we bring needless suffering upon ourselves and our families.

Do you seek spiritual abundance that can be yours through the person of God's only begotten Son? Then invite Christ into your heart and live according to His teachings. And, when you confront a difficult decision or a powerful temptation, seek

99 QUESTIONS—GOD'S ANSWERS FOR DADS

God's wisdom and trust it. When you do, you will receive untold blessings—not only for this day, but also for all eternity.

Life is a series of choices between the bad, the good, and the best. Everything depends on how we choose.

Vance Havner

Every day, I find countless opportunities to decide whether I will obey God and demonstrate my love for Him or try to please myself or the world system. God is waiting for my choices.

Bill Bright

Just as no one can go to hell or heaven for me, so no one can believe for me and so no one can open or close heaven or hell for me, and no one can drive me either to believe or disbelieve.

Martin Luther

A PRAYER FOR DADS

Heavenly Father, I have many choices to make. Help me choose wisely as I follow in the footsteps of Your only begotten Son. Amen

? QUESTION 14

Our family has so much to be thankful for. What should we do?

THE QUICK ANSWER

Don't overlook God's gifts: Every sunrise represents yet another beautifully wrapped gift from God. Unwrap it; treasure it; use it; and give thanks to the Giver.

Saying "Thanks" to God

Give thanks in all circumstances;
for this is God's will for you in Christ Jesus.
1 Thessalonians 5:18 NIV

The words of 1 Thessalonians 5:18 remind us to give thanks in every circumstance of life. But sometimes, when our hearts are troubled and our spirits are crushed, we don't feel like celebrating. Yet even when the clouds of despair darken our lives, God offers us His love, His strength, and His grace. And as believers, we must thank Him.

Have you thanked God today for blessings that are too numerous to count? Have you offered Him your heartfelt prayers and your wholehearted praise? If not, it's time to slow down and offer a prayer of thanksgiving to the One who has given you life on earth and life eternal.

No matter our circumstances, we owe God so much more than we can ever repay, and the least we can do is to thank Him.

We ought to give thanks for all fortune: if it is good, because it is good, if bad, because it works in us patience, humility, and the contempt of this world along with the hope of our eternal country.

C. S. Lewis

The words "thank" and "think" come from the same root word. If we would think more, we would thank more.

Warren Wiersbe

It is only with gratitude that life becomes rich.

Dietrich Bonhoeffer

A PRAYER FOR DADS

Lord, You have blessed me with a loving family—make me a father who is thankful, loving, responsible, and wise. I praise You, Father, for the gift of Your Son and for the gift of salvation. Let me be a joyful Christian and a worthy example, this day and every day that I live. Amen

QUESTION 15

What does God's Word say about work?

THE QUICK ANSWER

Work is honored by God—He expects each of us to do our fair share. So encourage your children to find meaningful work that they enjoy. People who are passionate about their professions are usually more successful than people who aren't.

Getting the Work Done

Do not be lazy but work hard, serving the Lord with all your heart.
Romans 12:11 NCV

Providing for your family requires work and lots of it. And as a hardworking dad, you have earned the gratitude of your loved ones and the praise of your Heavenly Father.

It has been said that there are no shortcuts to any place worth going. Dads agree. Making the grade in today's competitive workplace is not easy. In fact, it can be very difficult indeed. But, even when the workday is long and the workload is difficult, we must not become discouraged.

God did not create us for lives of mediocrity; He created us for far greater things. Earning great things usually requires determination, persistence, and hard work—which is perfectly fine with God. After all, He knows that we're up to the task, and He has big plans for us. Very big plans.

Chiefly the mold of a man's fortune is in his own hands.

Francis Bacon

People who work for money only are usually miserable, because there is no fulfillment and no meaning to what they do.

Dave Ramsey

If you want to reach your potential, you need to add a strong work ethic to your talent.

John Maxwell

It may be that the day of judgment will dawn tomorrow; in that case, we shall gladly stop working for a better tomorrow. But not before.

Dietrich Bonhoeffer

A PRAYER FOR DADS

Lord, let me be an industrious worker in Your fields. Those fields are ripe, Lord, and Your workers are few. Let me be counted as Your faithful, diligent servant today, and every day. Amen

Some things are very hard to accept. What should I do?

THE QUICK ANSWER

You must learn to accept the things you cannot change—since you can't change the past, you must learn to accept it. Otherwise, you'll make yourself miserable as you continually rehash yesterday's disappointments.

Accepting Life

The Lord says, "Forget what happened before, and do not think
about the past. Look at the new thing I am going to do.
It is already happening. Don't you see it?
I will make a road in the desert and rivers in the dry land."
Isaiah 43:18-19 NCV

Sometimes, we must accept life on its terms, not our own. Life has a way of unfolding, not as we will, but as it will. And sometimes, there is precious little we can do to change things.

When events transpire that are beyond our control, we have a choice: we can either learn the art of acceptance, or we can make ourselves miserable as we struggle to change the unchangeable.

We must entrust the things we cannot change to God. Once we have done so, we can prayerfully and faithfully tackle the important work that He has placed before us: doing something about the things we can change . . . and doing it sooner rather than later.

The one true way of dying to self is the way of patience, meekness, humility, and resignation to God.

Andrew Murray

Prayer may not get us what we want, but it will teach us to want what we need.

Vance Havner

Trust the past to God's mercy, the present to God's love, and the future to God's providence.

St. Augustine

A PRAYER FOR DADS

Dear Lord, let me live in the present, not the past. Let me focus on my blessings, not my sorrows. Give me the wisdom to be thankful for the gifts that I do have, and not bitter about the things that I don't have. Let me accept what was, let me give thanks for what is, and let me have faith in what most surely will be: the promise of eternal life with You. Amen

Sometimes life is difficult. When I'm fearful for myself or my family, what should I do?

THE QUICK ANSWER

Ask God for strength and wisdom. And above all, trust the Lord to solve problems that are simply too big for you to solve. When you turn everything over to God, you can live courageously.

Courage for Difficult Days

Be strong and courageous, and do the work. Do not be afraid or discouraged, for the Lord God, my God, is with you.
1 Chronicles 28:20 NIV

Being a godly father in this difficult world is no easy task. Ours is a time of uncertainty and danger, a time when even the most courageous dads have legitimate cause for concern. But as believers we can live courageously, knowing that we have been saved by a loving Father and His only begotten Son.

Are you anxious? Take those anxieties to God. Are you troubled? Take your troubles to Him. Does the world seem to be trembling beneath your feet? Seek protection from the One who cannot be moved. The same God who created the universe will protect you if you ask Him . . . so ask Him. And then live courageously, knowing that even in these troubled times, God is always as near as your next breath.

Take courage. We walk in the wilderness today and in the Promised Land tomorrow.

D. L. Moody

Do not let Satan deceive you into being afraid of God's plans for your life.

R. A. Torrey

Our Lord is searching for people who will make a difference. Christians dare not dissolve into the background or blend into the neutral scenery of the world.

Charles Swindoll

A PRAYER FOR DADS

Lord, at times, this world is a fearful place. I fear for my family and especially for my children. Yet, You have promised me that You are with me always. With You as my protector, I am not afraid. Today, Dear Lord, let me live courageously as I place my trust in You. Amen

? QUESTION 18

Is the Bible really God's Word, or is it simply another book?

THE QUICK ANSWER

The Bible is the best-selling book of all time . . . for good reason. Ruth Bell Graham, wife of evangelist Billy Graham, believes in the importance of God's Word: "The Reference Point for the Christian is the Bible. All values, judgments, and attitudes must be gauged in relationship to this Reference Point." Make certain that you're an avid reader of God's best-seller, and make sure that you keep reading it as long as you live!

Nourished by the Word

You will be a good servant of Christ Jesus,
constantly nourished on the words of the faith
and of the sound doctrine which you have been following.
1 Timothy 4:6 NASB

God's Word is unlike any other book. The Bible is a roadmap for life here on earth and for life eternal. As Christians, we are called upon to study God's Holy Word, to trust its promises, to follow its commandments, and to share its Good News with the world.

As believers, we must study the Bible and meditate upon its meaning for our lives. Otherwise, we deprive ourselves of a priceless gift from our Creator. God's Holy Word is, indeed, a transforming, life-changing, one-of-a-kind treasure. And, a passing acquaintance with the Good Book is insufficient for Christians who seek to obey God's Word and to understand His will. After all, neither man nor woman should live by bread alone . . .

————————————————

Reading news without reading the Bible will inevitably lead to an unbalanced life, an anxious spirit, a worried and depressed soul.

Bill Bright

It takes calm, thoughtful, prayerful meditation on the Word to extract its deepest nourishment.

Vance Havner

A PRAYER FOR DADS

Heavenly Father, Your Word is a light unto the world; I will study it and trust it and share it. In all that I do, help me be a worthy witness for You as I share the Good News of Your perfect Son and Your perfect Word. Amen

?QUESTION 19

What does the Bible say about my daily devotional?

THE QUICK ANSWER

Time and again, the Bible stresses the need to study God's Word every day, with no exceptions. If you make your morning devotional an ironclad habit, you'll be blessed.

Every Day with God

Morning by morning he wakens me and opens my understanding to his will. The Sovereign Lord has spoken to me, and I have listened.
Isaiah 50:4-5 NLT

Each new day is a gift from God, and if we are wise, we spend a few quiet moments each morning thanking the Giver. Daily life is woven together with the threads of habit, and no habit is more important to our spiritual health than the discipline of daily prayer and devotion to the Creator.

When we begin each day with heads bowed and hearts lifted, we remind ourselves of God's love, His protection, and His commandments. And if we are wise, we align our priorities for the coming day with the teachings and commandments that God has given us through His Holy Word.

Are you seeking to change some aspect of your life? Do you seek to improve the condition of your spiritual or physical health? If so, ask for God's help and ask for it many times each day . . . starting with your morning devotional.

We must appropriate the tender mercy of God every day after conversion or problems quickly develop. We need his grace daily in order to live a righteous life.

Jim Cymbala

I suggest you discipline yourself to spend time daily in a systematic reading of God's Word. Make this "quiet time" a priority that nobody can change.

Warren Wiersbe

A person with no devotional life generally struggles with faith and obedience.

Charles Stanley

A PRAYER FOR DADS

Lord, help me to hear Your direction for my life in the quiet moments when I study Your Holy Word. And as I go about my daily activities, let everything that I say and do be pleasing to You. Amen

?QUESTION 20

We live in a materialistic world. What does the Bible have to say about that?

THE QUICK ANSWER

Too much stuff doesn't ensure happiness. In fact, having too much stuff can actually prevent happiness.

Beyond Materialism

Don't collect for yourselves treasures on earth, where moth
and rust destroy and where thieves break in and steal.
But collect for yourselves treasures in heaven, where neither moth
nor rust destroys, and where thieves don't break in and steal.
For where your treasure is, there your heart will be also.
Matthew 6:19-21 Holman CSB

In our modern society, we need money to live. But as Christians, we must never make the acquisition of money the central focus of our lives. Money is a tool, but it should never overwhelm our sensibilities. The focus of life must be squarely on things spiritual, not in things material.

Whenever we place our love for material possessions above our love for God—or when we yield to the countless other temptations of everyday living—we find ourselves engaged in a struggle between good and evil, a clash between God and Satan. Our responses to these struggles have implications that echo throughout our families and throughout our communities. Let us choose wisely by freeing ourselves from that subtle yet powerful temptation: the temptation to love the world more than we love God.

When possessions become our god, we become materialistic and greedy . . . and we forfeit our contentment and our joy.

Charles Swindoll

A society that pursues pleasure runs the risk of raising expectations ever higher, so that true contentment always lies tantalizingly out of reach.

Philip Yancey and Paul Brand

A PRAYER FOR DADS

Lord, my greatest possession is my relationship with You through Jesus Christ. You have promised that, when I first seek Your kingdom and Your righteousness, You will give me whatever I need. Let me trust You completely, Lord, for my needs, both material and spiritual, this day and always. Amen

I've made plenty of mistakes, and I can't seem to make peace with the past. What should I do?

THE QUICK ANSWER

Everybody makes mistakes—wise people learn from them. And remember that the past is past, so don't live there. If you're focused on the past, change your focus. If you're living in the past, it's time to stop living there (Isaiah 43:18-19).

Beyond the Mistakes

*Instead, God has chosen the world's foolish things
to shame the wise, and God has chosen the world's
weak things to shame the strong.*
1 Corinthians 1:27 Holman CSB

As parents, we are far from perfect. And, without question, our children are imperfect as well. Thus, we are imperfect parents raising imperfect children, and, as a result, mistakes are bound to happen.

Has someone in your family experienced a recent setback? If so, it's time to start looking for the lesson that God is trying to teach. It's time to learn what needs to be learned, change what needs to be changed, and move on.

You and your loved ones should view mistakes as opportunities to reassess God's will for your lives. And while you're at it, you should consider life's inevitable disappointments to be powerful opportunities to learn more—more about yourselves, more about your circumstances, and more about your world.

Truth will sooner come out of error than from confusion.

Francis Bacon

Lord, when we are wrong, make us willing to change; and when we are right, make us easy to live with.

Peter Marshall

Very few things motivate us to give God our undivided attention like being faced with the negative consequences of our decisions.

Charles Stanley

A PRAYER FOR DADS

Dear Lord, there's a right way to do things and a wrong way to do things. When I do things that are wrong, help me be quick to ask for forgiveness . . . and quick to correct my mistakes. Amen

If I want God to guide me, what should I do?

THE QUICK ANSWER

If you want God's guidance, ask for it. When you pray for guidance, God will give it.

God's Guidance

Every morning he wakes me. He teaches me to listen like a student.
The Lord God helps me learn . . . .
Isaiah 50:4-5 NCV

The Bible promises that God will guide you if you let Him. Your job, of course, is to let Him. But sometimes, you will be tempted to do otherwise. Sometimes, you'll be tempted to go along with the crowd; other times, you'll be tempted to do things your way, not God's way. When you feel those temptations, resist them.

What will you allow to guide you through the coming day: your own desires (or, for that matter, the desires of your friends)? Or will you allow God to lead the way? The answer should be obvious. You should let God be your guide. When you entrust your life to Him completely and without reservation, God will give you the strength to meet any challenge, the courage to face any trial, and the wisdom to live in His righteousness. So trust Him today and seek His guidance. When you do, your next step will be the right one.

Fix your eyes upon the Lord! Do it once. Do it daily. Do it constantly. Look at the Lord and keep looking at Him.

Charles Swindoll

God's plan for our guidance is for us to grow gradually in wisdom before we get to the crossroads.

Bill Hybels

We must always invite Jesus to be the navigator of our plans, desires, wills, and emotions, for He is the way, the truth, and the life.

Bill Bright

A PRAYER FOR DADS

Dear Lord, thank You for Your constant presence and Your constant love. I draw near to You this day with the confidence that You are ready to guide me. Help me walk closely with You, Father, and help me share Your Good News with all who cross my path. Amen

? **QUESTION 23**

If I feel guilty about something, what should I do?

THE QUICK ANSWER

First, make sure that you're no longer doing the thing that caused your guilt in the first place. Then, ask for forgiveness (from God and from anybody you've hurt). Next, make sure to forgive yourself. And finally, if you still have residual feelings of bitterness or regret, keep asking God to cleanse your heart. When you ask, He will answer in His own time and in His own way.

Beyond Guilt

There is therefore now no condemnation to those who
are in Christ Jesus, who do not walk according to the flesh,
but according to the Spirit.
Romans 8:1 NKJV

All of us have made mistakes. Sometimes our failures result from our own shortsightedness. On other occasions, we are swept up in events that are beyond our abilities to control. Under either set of circumstances, we may experience intense feelings of guilt. But God has an answer for the guilt that we feel. That answer, of course, is His forgiveness.

When we ask our Heavenly Father for His forgiveness, He forgives us completely and without reservation. Then, we must do the difficult work of forgiving ourselves in the same way that God has forgiven us: thoroughly and unconditionally.

If you're feeling guilty, then it's time for a special kind of housecleaning—a housecleaning of your mind and your heart . . . beginning NOW!

Guilt is a gift that leads us to grace.

Franklin Graham

Identify the sin. Confess it. Turn from it. Avoid it at all costs. Live with a clean, forgiven conscience. Don't dwell on what God has forgotten!

Max Lucado

Satan wants you to feel guilty. Your Heavenly Father wants you to know that you are forgiven.

Warren Wiersbe

A PRAYER FOR DADS

Dear Lord, thank You for the guilt that I feel when I disobey You. Help me confess my wrongdoings, help me accept Your forgiveness, and help me renew my passion to serve You. Amen

Sometimes, I know the thing that needs to be done, but taking action is hard. What should I do?

THE QUICK ANSWER

Pray as if everything depended upon God, and work as if everything depended on you.

Getting It Done Now

When you make a vow to God, don't delay fulfilling it, because He does not delight in fools. Fulfill what you vow.
Ecclesiastes 5:4 Holman CSB

The old saying is both familiar and true: actions speak louder than words. And as believers, we must beware: our actions should always give credence to the changes that Christ can make in the lives of those who walk with Him.

God calls upon each of us to act in accordance with His will and with respect for His commandments. If we are to be responsible believers, we must realize that it is never enough simply to hear the instructions of God; we must also live by them. And it is never enough to wait idly by while others do God's work here on earth; we, too, must act. Doing God's work is a responsibility that each of us must bear, and when we do, our loving Heavenly Father rewards our efforts with a bountiful harvest.

Do noble things, do not dream them all day long.

Charles Kingsley

Now is the only time worth having because, indeed, it is the only time we have.

C. H. Spurgeon

Every time you refuse to face up to life and its problems, you weaken your character.

E. Stanley Jones

Give to us clear vision that we may know where to stand and what to stand for. Let us not be content to wait and see what will happen, but give us the determination to make the right things happen.

Peter Marshall

A PRAYER FOR DADS

Dear Lord, today is a new day. Help me tackle the important tasks immediately, even if those tasks are unpleasant. Don't let me put off until tomorrow what I should do today. Amen

?QUESTION 25

What does the Bible say about the way I should manage my time? And what about the amount of time I spend with my family?

THE QUICK ANSWER

The Bible warns us that there's no time to waste. Every day—indeed every moment—is precious.

Time for Family

We can't afford to waste a minute, must not squander these precious daylight hours in frivolity and indulgence, in sleeping around and dissipation, in bickering and grabbing everything in sight. Get out of bed and get dressed! Don't loiter and linger, waiting until the very last minute. Dress yourselves in Christ, and be up and about!
Romans 13:13-14 MSG

It takes time to build strong family ties . . . lots of time. Yet we live in a world where time seems to be an ever-shrinking commodity as we rush from place to place with seldom a moment to spare.

Has the busy pace of life robbed you of sufficient time with your loved ones? If so, it's time to fine-tune your priorities. And God can help.

When you make God a full partner in every aspect of your life, He will lead you along the proper path: His path. When you allow God to reign over your life, He will enrich your relationships and your life. So, as you plan for the day ahead, make God's priorities your priorities. When you do, every other priority will have a tendency to fall neatly into place.

I don't buy the cliché that quality time is the most important thing. If you don't have enough quantity, you won't get quality.

Leighton Ford

The more time you give to something, the more you reveal its importance and value to you.

Rick Warren

What really builds togetherness is time spent together—lots of time.

Dennis Swanberg

A PRAYER FOR DADS

Dear Lord, You have given me a wonderful gift: time here on earth. Let me use it wisely—for the glory of Your kingdom and the betterment of my family—today and every day that I live. Amen

What does the Bible say about following in Jesus' footsteps?

THE QUICK ANSWER

If you want to follow in Christ's footsteps . . . welcome Him into your heart, obey His commandments, and share His never-ending love.

Follow Him

"Follow Me," Jesus told them, "and I will make you into fishers of men!" Immediately they left their nets and followed Him.
Mark 1:17-18 Holman CSB

Whom will you walk with today? Will you walk with people who worship the ways of the world? Or will you walk with the Son of God?

Jesus walks with you. Are you walking with Him? Hopefully, you will choose to walk with Him today and every day of your life.

Jesus has called upon believers of every generation (and that includes you) to follow in His footsteps. And God's Word promises that when you follow in Christ's footsteps, you will learn how to live freely and lightly (Matthew 11:28-30).

Are you worried about the day ahead? Be confident in God's power. He will never desert you. Are you concerned about the future? Be courageous and call upon God. He will protect you. Are you confused? Listen to the quiet voice of your Heavenly Father. He is not a God of confusion. Talk with God; listen to Him; follow His commandments . . . and walk with His Son—starting now.

Our responsibility is to feed from Him, to stay close to Him, to follow Him—because sheep easily go astray—so that we eternally experience the protection and companionship of our Great Shepherd the Lord Jesus Christ.

Franklin Graham

We have in Jesus Christ a perfect example of how to put God's truth into practice.

Bill Bright

A PRAYER FOR DADS

Dear Lord, You sent Jesus to save the world and to save me. I thank You for Jesus, and I will do my best to follow Him, today and forever. Amen

Sometimes my life doesn't seem very exciting. Why should I be excited about life?

THE QUICK ANSWER

Today is a cause for celebration. Plan your day—and your life—accordingly.

Celebrate!

Celebrate God all day, every day. I mean, revel in him!
Philippians 4:4 MSG

Are you a dad who celebrates life? Hopefully you are! God has richly blessed you, and He wants you to rejoice in His gifts.

God fills each day to the brim with possibilities, and He challenges each of us to use our gifts for the glory of His kingdom. When we honor the Father and place Him at the center of our lives, every day becomes a cause for celebration.

Today is a non-renewable resource—once it's gone, it's gone forever. Our responsibility—both as fathers and as believers—is to use this day in the service of God's will and in the service of His people. When we do so, we enrich our own lives and the lives of those whom we love. And the Father smiles.

99 QUESTIONS—GOD'S ANSWERS FOR DADS

Let God have you, and let God love you—and don't be surprised if your heart begins to hear music you've never heard and your feet learn to dance as never before.

Max Lucado

Some of us seem so anxious about avoiding hell that we forget to celebrate our journey toward heaven.

Philip Yancey

Joy is the great note all throughout the Bible.

Oswald Chambers

If you can forgive the person you were, accept the person you are, and believe in the person you will become, you are headed for joy. So celebrate your life.

Barbara Johnson

A PRAYER FOR DADS

Dear Lord, You have given me so many reasons to celebrate. Today, let me choose an attitude of cheerfulness. Let me be a joyful Christian, Lord, quick to laugh and slow to anger. Let me praise You, Lord, and give thanks for Your blessings. Today is Your creation; let me celebrate it . . . and You. Amen

QUESTION 28

What does the Bible say about optimism?

THE QUICK ANSWER

The Bible promises that if you give your heart to Jesus, your eternal future is secure. So even when times are tough, you can be hopeful, joyful, and optimistic.

Optimism Now

I can do everything through him that gives me strength.
Philippians 4:13 NIV

The words of Psalm 118:24 remind us of a profound yet simple truth: "This is the day which the LORD hath made; we will rejoice and be glad in it" (KJV).

As each day unfolds, we are literally surrounded by more opportunities than we can count—opportunities to improve our own lives and the lives of those we love. God's Word promises that each of us possess the ability to experience earthly peace and spiritual abundance.

So, as we face the inevitable challenges of life here on earth, we must not become discouraged. We must, instead, arm ourselves with the promises of God and when we do, we can expect the very best that life—and God—has to offer.

The popular idea of faith is of a certain obstinate optimism: the hope, tenaciously held in the face of trouble, that the universe is fundamentally friendly and things may get better.

J. I. Packer

Christ can put a spring in your step and a thrill in your heart. Optimism and cheerfulness are products of knowing Christ.

Billy Graham

The essence of optimism is that it takes no account of the present, but it is a source of inspiration, of vitality, and of hope. Where others have resigned, it enables a man to hold his head high, to claim the future for himself, and not abandon it to his enemy.

Dietrich Bonhoeffer

A PRAYER FOR DADS

Lord, You care for me, You love me, and You have given me the priceless gift of eternal life through Your Son Jesus. Because of You, Lord, I have every reason to live each day with celebration and hope. Help me to face this day with a spirit of optimism and thanksgiving so that I may lift the spirits of those I meet as I share the Good News of Your Son. And, let me focus my thoughts on You and Your incomparable gifts today and forever. Amen

? QUESTION 29

How best can I teach my children the importance of self-discipline?

THE QUICK ANSWER

If you want to teach discipline, you must be disciplined in your own approach to life. You can't teach it if you won't live it.

The Rewards of Discipline

Discipline yourself for the purpose of godliness.
1 Timothy 4:7 NASB

Wise fathers teach their children the importance of discipline using both words and examples. Disciplined dads understand that God doesn't reward laziness or misbehavior. To the contrary, God expects His believers to lead lives that are above reproach. And, He punishes those who disobey His commandments.

In Proverbs 28:19, God's message is clear: "He who works his land will have abundant food, but the one who chases fantasies will have his fill of poverty" (NIV). When we work diligently and consistently, we can expect a bountiful harvest.

But we must never expect the harvest to precede the labor. First, we must lead lives of discipline and obedience; then, we will reap the never-ending rewards that God has promised.

Work is doing it. Discipline is doing it every day. Diligence is doing it well every day.

Dave Ramsey

As we seek to become disciples of Jesus Christ, we should never forget that the word *disciple* is directly related to the word *discipline*. To be a disciple of the Lord Jesus Christ is to know his discipline.

Dennis Swanberg

Discipline is training that develops and corrects.

Charles Stanley

A PRAYER FOR DADS

Lord, let me be a disciplined parent, and let me teach my children to lead disciplined lives. Let me be Your faithful servant, Lord, and let me teach faithfulness by my conduct and by my communications. Let me raise my family in the knowledge of Your Word, and let me follow Your commandments just as surely as I teach my children to obey You and to love You. Amen

I have big dreams. What should I do about them?

THE QUICK ANSWER

Making your dreams come true requires work. John Maxwell writes "The gap between your vision and your present reality can only be filled through a commitment to maximize your potential." Enough said.

Big Dreams

Live full lives, full in the fullness of God. God can do anything, you know–far more than you could ever imagine or guess or request in your wildest dreams! He does it not by pushing us around but by working within us, his Spirit deeply and gently within us.
Ephesians 3:19-20 MSG

Are you willing to entertain the possibility that God has big plans in store for you and your family? Hopefully so. Yet sometimes, especially if you've recently experienced a life-altering disappointment, you may find it difficult to envision a brighter future for yourself and your family. If so, it's time to reconsider your own capabilities . . . and God's.

Your Heavenly Father created you with unique gifts and untapped talents; your job is to tap them. When you do, you'll begin to feel an increasing sense of confidence in yourself and in your future.

It takes courage to dream big dreams. You will discover that courage when you do three things: accept the past, trust God to handle the future, and make the most of the time He has given you today.

Nothing is too difficult for God, and no dreams are too big for Him—not even yours. So start living—and dreaming—accordingly.

Allow your dreams a place in your prayers and plans. God-given dreams can help you move into the future He is preparing for you.

Barbara Johnson

Sometimes our dreams were so big that it took two people to dream them.

Marie T. Freeman

A PRAYER FOR DADS

Dear Lord, give me the courage to dream and the faithfulness to trust in Your perfect plan. When I am worried or weary, give me strength for today and hope for tomorrow. Keep me mindful of Your healing power, Your infinite love, and Your eternal salvation. Amen

? QUESTION 31

What does the Bible have to say about the importance of being a joyful person?

THE QUICK ANSWER

God's Word instructs us to be joyful. And we must remember that joy does not depend upon our circumstances, but upon our relationship with God.

Real Joy

I've told you these things for a purpose: that my joy might be your joy, and your joy wholly mature.
John 15:11 MSG

Are you a dad whose joy is evident for all to see? If so, congratulations: you're doing God's will. Psalm 100 reminds us that, as believers, we have every reason to celebrate: "Shout for joy to the LORD, all the earth. Worship the LORD with gladness" (vv. 1-2 NIV). Yet sometimes, amid the inevitable hustle and bustle of life here on earth, we can forfeit—albeit temporarily—the joy that God intends for our lives.

If you find yourself feeling discouraged or worse, it's time to slow down and have a quiet conversation with your Creator. If your heart is heavy, open the door of your soul to the Father and to His only begotten Son. Christ offers you His peace and His joy. Accept it and share it freely, just as Christ has freely shared His joy with you.

Joy comes from knowing God loves me and knows who I am and where I'm going . . . that my future is secure as I rest in Him.

James Dobson

I choose joy. I will refuse the temptation to be cynical; cynicism is the tool of a lazy thinker. I will refuse to see people as anything less than human beings, created by God. I will refuse to see any problem as anything less than an opportunity to see God.

Max Lucado

Joy is the direct result of having God's perspective on our daily lives and the effect of loving our Lord enough to obey His commands and trust His promises.

Bill Bright

A PRAYER FOR DADS

Dear Lord, You have blessed me with a loving family; make me thankful, loving, responsible, and wise. I praise You, Father, for the gift of Your Son and for the gift of salvation. Let me be a joyful Christian and a worthy example, this day and every day that I live. Amen

Sometimes I'm tempted to give up. What advice does the Bible have for me?

THE QUICK ANSWER

The world encourages instant gratification but God's work takes time. So remember the words of C. H. Spurgeon: "By perseverance, the snail reached the ark."

The Power of Perseverance

For you need endurance, so that after you have done God's will,
you may receive what was promised.
Hebrews 10:36 Holman CSB

The occasional disappointments and failures of life are inevitable. Such setbacks are simply the price that we must pay for our willingness to take risks as we follow our dreams. But even when we encounter setbacks, we must never lose faith.

The reassuring words of Hebrews 10:36 serve as a comforting reminder that perseverance indeed pays: "You have need of endurance, so that when you have done the will of God, you may receive what was promised" (NASB).

Are you willing to trust God's Word? And are you willing to keep "fighting the good fight," even when you've experienced unexpected difficulties? If so, you may soon be surprised at the creative ways that God finds to help determined people like you . . . people who possess the wisdom and the courage to persevere.

Perseverance is more than endurance. It is endurance combined with absolute assurance and certainty that what we are looking for is going to happen.

Oswald Chambers

In the Bible, patience is not a passive acceptance of circumstances. It is a courageous perseverance in the face of suffering and difficulty.

Warren Wiersbe

A PRAYER FOR DADS

Lord, when life is difficult, I am tempted to abandon hope in the future. But You are my God, and I can draw strength from You. Let me trust You, Father, in good times and in bad times. Let me persevere—even if my soul is troubled—and let me follow Your Son Jesus Christ this day and forever. Amen

Sometimes, it's easy for me to become angry. What does the Bible say about anger?

THE QUICK ANSWER

The Bible warns us time and again that anger is only one letter away from danger. So the next time you're tempted to lose your cool, walk away before you get carried away.

Beyond Anger

But now you must also put away all the following: anger, wrath, malice, slander, and filthy language from your mouth.
Colossians 3:8 Holman CSB

The frustrations of everyday living can sometimes get the better of us, and we allow minor disappointments to cause us major problems. When we allow ourselves to become overly irritated by the inevitable ups and downs of life, we become overstressed, overheated, over-anxious, and just plain angry.

When you allow yourself to become angry, you are certain to defeat at least one person: yourself. When you allow the minor frustrations of everyday life to hijack your emotions, you do harm to yourself and to your loved ones. So today and every day, guard yourself against the kind of angry thinking that inevitably takes a toll on your emotions and your relationships.

As the old saying goes, "Anger usually improves nothing but the arch of a cat's back." So don't allow feelings of anger or frustration to rule your life, or, for that matter, your day—your life is simply too short for that, and you deserve much better treatment than that . . . from yourself.

———————————

Anger is the noise of the soul; the unseen irritant of the heart; the relentless invader of silence.

Max Lucado

When you strike out in anger, you may miss the other person, but you will always hit yourself.

Jim Gallery

Bitterness and anger, usually over trivial things, make havoc of homes, churches, and friendships.

Warren Wiersbe

A PRAYER FOR DADS

Lord, sometimes, it is so easy to lose my temper and my perspective. When anger burdens my soul, enable me to calm myself and to be a witness to Your truth and righteousness. Let my children see me as a model of kindness and forgiveness, today and every day. Amen

QUESTION 34

What does the Bible say about prayer?

THE QUICK ANSWER

Pray early and often: One way to make sure that your heart is in tune with God is to pray often. The more you talk to the Father, the more He will talk to you.

Too Busy to Pray?

If my people who are called by my name, will humble themselves and pray and seek my face and turn from their wicked ways, then will I hear from heaven and will forgive their sin and will heal their land.

2 Chronicles 7:14 NIV

Does your family pray together often, or just at church? Are you a little band of prayer warriors, or have you retreated from God's battlefield? Do you and yours pray only at mealtimes, or do you pray much more often than that? The answer to these questions will determine, to a surprising extent, the level of your family's spiritual health.

Jesus made it clear to His disciples: they should pray always. And so should you. Genuine, heartfelt prayer changes things and it changes you. When you lift your heart to the Father, you open yourself to a never-ending source of divine wisdom and infinite love.

Your family's prayers are powerful. So, as you go about your daily activities, remember God's instructions: "Rejoice always! Pray constantly. Give thanks in everything, for this is God's will for you in Christ Jesus" (1 Thessalonians 5:16-18 Holman CSB). Start praying in the morning and keep praying until you fall off to sleep at night. And rest assured: God is always listening, and He always wants to hear from you and your family.

———————————

Prayer connects us with God's limitless potential.

Henry Blackaby

God wants to remind us that nothing on earth or in hell can ultimately stand against the man or the woman who calls on the name of the Lord!

Jim Cymbala

A PRAYER FOR DADS

Dear Lord, I will open my heart to You. I will take my concerns, my fears, my plans, and my hopes to You in prayer. And, then, I will trust the answers that You give. You are my loving Father, and I will accept Your will for my life today and every day that I live. Amen

? QUESTION 35

I want to become a wiser, more thoughtful person. Where can I go to find wisdom?

THE QUICK ANSWER

If you own a Bible, you have ready access to God's wisdom. Your job is to read, to understand, and to apply His teachings to your life . . . starting now and ending never.

Wisdom Now!

Do you want to be counted wise, to build a reputation for wisdom?
Here's what you do: Live well, live wisely, live humbly.
It's the way you live, not the way you talk, that counts.
James 3:13 MSG

Do you seek wisdom for yourself and for your family? Of course you do. But as a savvy dad, you know that wisdom can be an elusive commodity in today's troubled world. In a society filled with temptations and distractions, it's easy for parents and children alike to stray far from the source of the ultimate wisdom: God's Holy Word.

When you begin a daily study of God's Word and live according to His commandments, you will become wise . . . in time. But don't expect to open your Bible today and be wise tomorrow. Wisdom is not like a mushroom; it does not spring up overnight. It is, instead, like an oak tree that starts as a tiny acorn, grows into a sapling, and eventually reaches up to the sky, tall and strong.

Today and every day, as a way of understanding God's plan for your life, study His Word and live by it. When you do, you will accumulate a storehouse of wisdom that will enrich your own life and the lives of your family members, your friends, and the world.

The more wisdom enters our hearts, the more we will be able to trust our hearts in difficult situations.

John Eldredge

If you lack knowledge, go to school. If you lack wisdom, get on your knees.

Vance Havner

A PRAYER FOR DADS

Dear Lord, give me wisdom to love my family, to care for them, and to help them understand the wisdom of Your Holy Word. Let me share Your wisdom by the words I speak and the example that I set, today and every day that I live. Amen

QUESTION 36

What does the Bible say about the example that I should set for my family?

THE QUICK ANSWER

Your life is a sermon. The words you choose to speak may have some impact on others, but not nearly as much impact as the life you choose to live. God wants you to be a positive role model to your family, to your friends, and to the world.

What Kind of Example?

You should be an example to the believers in speech, in conduct, in love, in faith, in purity.
1 Timothy 4:12 Holman CSB

Our children learn from the lessons we teach and the lives we live, but not necessarily in that order. As fathers, we serve as unforgettable role models for our children and our grandchildren. The lives we lead and the choices we make should serve as enduring examples of the spiritual abundance that is available to all who worship God and obey His commandments.

Are you God's obedient servant? Is your faith in Christ clearly demonstrated by the example that you set for your children? If so, you will be blessed by God, and so, of course, will they.

We urgently need people who encourage and inspire us to move toward God and away from the world's enticing pleasures.

Jim Cymbala

A holy life will produce the deepest impression. Lighthouses blow no horns; they only shine.

D. L. Moody

In our faith we follow in someone's steps. In our faith we leave footprints to guide others. It's the principle of discipleship.

Max Lucado

Our walk counts far more than our talk, always!

George Mueller

A PRAYER FOR DADS

Lord, make me a worthy example to my family and friends. And, let my words and my deeds serve as a testimony to the changes You have made in my life. Let me praise You, Father, by following in the footsteps of Your Son, and let others see Him through me. Amen

?QUESTION 37

I know I should be kind to other people, but sometimes it's so easy to overlook the needs of others. What does the Bible instruct me to do?

THE QUICK ANSWER

You can't just talk about it: In order to be a kind person, you must not only think kind thoughts, you must also do kind things. So get busy! The time to be kind is now.

Kindness Is a Choice

A kind man benefits himself,
but a cruel man brings disaster on himself.
Proverbs 11:17 Holman CSB

Christ showed His love for us by willingly sacrificing His own life so that we might have eternal life: "But God demonstrates his own love for us in this: While we were still sinners, Christ died for us" (Romans 5:8 NIV). We, as Christ's followers, are challenged to share His love with kind words on our lips and praise in our hearts.

Just as Christ has been—and will always be—the ultimate friend to His flock, so should we be Christlike in the kindness and generosity that we show toward others, especially those who are most in need.

When we walk each day with Jesus—and obey the commandments found in God's Holy Word—we become worthy ambassadors for Christ. When we share the love of Christ, we share a priceless gift with the world. As His servants, we must do no less.

Be so preoccupied with good will that you haven't room for ill will.

E. Stanley Jones

When you extend hospitality to others, you're not trying to impress people, you're trying to reflect God to them.

Max Lucado

When you launch an act of kindness out into the crosswinds of life, it will blow kindness back to you.

Dennis Swanberg

A PRAYER FOR DADS

Help me, Lord, to see the needs of those around me. Today, let me show courtesy to those who cross my path. Today, let me spread kind words in honor of Your Son. Today, let forgiveness rule my heart. And every day, Lord, let my love for Christ be demonstrated through the acts of kindness that I offer to those who need the healing touch of the Master's hand. Amen

I have challenges that seem overwhelming at times. What should I do?

THE QUICK ANSWER

Remember that whatever the size of your challenge, God is bigger. Trust Him to solve the problems that are simply too big for you tackle.

God Can Handle It

Cast your burden on the Lord, and He will support you;
He will never allow the righteous to be shaken.
Psalm 55:22 Holman CSB

It's a promise that is made over and over again in the Bible: Whatever "it" is, God can handle it.

Life isn't always easy. Far from it! Sometimes, life can be very, very difficult, indeed. But even when the storm clouds form overhead, even during our darkest moments, we're protected by a loving Heavenly Father.

When we're worried, God can reassure us; when we're sad, God can comfort us. When our hearts are broken, God is not just near; He is here. So we must lift our thoughts and prayers to Him. When we do, He will answer our prayers. Why?

Because He is our Shepherd, and He has promised to protect us now and forever.

The next time you're disappointed, don't panic. Don't give up. Just be patient and let God remind you he's still in control.

Max Lucado

We do not understand the intricate pattern of the stars in their course, but we know that He Who created them does, and that just as surely as He guides them, He is charting a safe course for us.

Billy Graham

You may not know what you are going to do; you only know that God knows what He is going to do.

Oswald Chambers

A PRAYER FOR DADS

Dear Lord, You rule over our world, and I will allow You to rule over my heart. I will obey Your commandments, I will study Your Word, and I will seek Your will for my life, today and every day of my life. Amen

QUESTION 39

What does the Bible say about my children?

THE QUICK ANSWER

The Bible says that your children are a gift from God. And that's precisely how you should treat them!

A Priceless Treasure: Your Children

Children are a gift from the LORD; they are a reward from him.
Psalm 127:4 NLT

We are aware that God has entrusted us with priceless treasures from above—our children. Every child is a glorious gift from the Father. And, with the Father's gift comes profound responsibilities. Thoughtful parents understand the critical importance of raising their children with love, with family, with discipline, and with God.

If you're lucky enough to be a father, give thanks to God for the gift of your child. Whether you're the father of a newborn or a seasoned granddad, remember this: your child—like every child—is a child of God. May you, as a responsible father, behave accordingly.

A child's life ought to be a child's life, full of simplicity.

Oswald Chambers

Happy is the child who happens in upon his parent from time to time to see him on his knees, or going aside regularly, to keep times with the Lord.

Larry Christenson

Our primary responsibility is to be sure our children grow up in homes where God is honored and the love of Christ reigns.

Billy Graham

No other structure can replace the family. Without it, our children have no moral foundation. Without it, they become moral illiterates whose only law is self.

Chuck Colson

A PRAYER FOR DADS

Thank You, Lord, for the priceless gift of my children. Because I am theirs and they are mine, I am blessed beyond words. Let me always be mindful of the profound responsibilities of parenthood, and let me raise my children to know You and to walk with You always. Amen

How should I respond to Jesus' sacrifice on the cross?

THE QUICK ANSWER

Jesus made an incredible sacrifice for you. Now, it's your turn to respond to Christ's sacrifice by turning your heart and your soul over to Him.

Considering the Cross

But as for me, I will never boast about anything
except the cross of our Lord Jesus Christ, through whom the world
has been crucified to me, and I to the world.
Galatians 6:14 Holman CSB

As we consider Christ's sacrifice on the cross, we should be profoundly humbled and profoundly grateful. And today, as we come to Christ in prayer, we should do so in a spirit of quiet, heartfelt devotion to the One who gave His life so that we might have life eternal.

He was the Son of God, but He wore a crown of thorns. He was the Savior of mankind, yet He was put to death on a rough-hewn cross made of wood. He offered His healing touch to an unsaved world, and yet the same hands that had healed the sick and raised the dead were pierced with nails.

Christ humbled Himself on a cross—for you. He shed His blood—for you. He has offered to walk with you through this life and throughout all eternity. As you approach Him today in prayer, think about His sacrifice and His grace. And be humble.

No man understands the Scriptures unless he is acquainted with the cross.

Martin Luther

There is no detour to holiness. Jesus came to the resurrection through the cross, not around it.

Leighton Ford

It was not the soldiers who killed him, nor the screams of the mob: It was his devotion to us.

Max Lucado

A PRAYER FOR DADS

Dear Jesus, You are my Savior and my protector. You suffered on the cross for me, and I will give You honor and praise every day of my life. I will honor You with my words, my thoughts, and my prayers. And I will live according to Your commandments, so that thorough me, others might come to know Your perfect love. Amen

What does the Bible teach us about praising God?

THE QUICK ANSWER

Praise Him! One of the main reasons you and your family go to church is to praise God. But, you need not wait until Sunday rolls around to thank your Heavenly Father. Instead, you can praise Him many times each day by saying silent prayers that only He can hear.

Time to Praise God

I will praise you, Lord, with all my heart. I will tell all the miracles you have done. I will be happy because of you; God Most High, I will sing praises to your name.

Psalm 9:1-2 NCV

When is the best time to praise God? In church? Before dinner is served? When we tuck little children into bed? None of the above. The best time to praise God is all day, every day, to the greatest extent we can, with thanksgiving in our hearts.

Too many of us, even well-intentioned believers, tend to "compartmentalize" our waking hours into a few familiar categories: work, rest, play, family time, and worship. To do so is a mistake. Worship and praise should be woven into the fabric of everything we do; it should never be relegated to a weekly three-hour visit to church on Sunday morning.

Mrs. Charles E. Cowman, the author of the classic devotional text, *Streams in the Desert*, wrote, "Two wings are necessary to lift our souls toward God: prayer and praise. Prayer asks. Praise accepts the answer." Today, find a little more time to lift your concerns to God in prayer, and praise Him for all that He has done. He's listening . . . and He wants to hear from you.

Be not afraid of saying too much in the praises of God; all the danger is of saying too little.

Matthew Henry

Praise opens the window of our hearts, preparing us to walk more closely with God. Prayer raises the window of our spirit, enabling us to listen more clearly to the Father.

Max Lucado

A PRAYER FOR DADS

Heavenly Father, I come to You today with hope in my heart and praise on my lips. Make me a faithful steward of the blessings You have entrusted to me. Let me follow in Christ's footsteps today and every day that I live. And let my words and deeds praise You now and forever. Amen

? QUESTION 42

Sometimes it's hard for me to forgive the people who have hurt me. What does the Bible say about that?

THE QUICK ANSWER

God's Word instructs you to forgive others . . . no exceptions. Forgiveness is its own reward and bitterness is its own punishment. So guard your words and your thoughts accordingly.

Forgiveness Now

*Then Peter came to him and asked, "Lord, how often should
I forgive someone who sins against me? Seven times?"
"No!" Jesus replied, "seventy times seven!"*
Matthew 18:21-22 NLT

Even the most mild-mannered dads will, on occasion, have reason to become angry with the shortcomings of family members and friends. But wise dads are quick to forgive others, just as God has forgiven them.

Forgiveness is God's commandment, but oh how difficult a commandment it can be to follow. Being frail, fallible, imperfect human beings, we are quick to anger, quick to blame, slow to forgive, and even slower to forget. No matter. Forgiveness, no matter how difficult, is God's way, and it must be our way, too.

If, in your heart, you hold bitterness against even a single person, forgive. If there exists even one person, alive or dead, whom you have not forgiven, follow God's commandment and His will for your life: forgive. If you are embittered against yourself for some past mistake or shortcoming, forgive. Then, to the best of your abilities, forget. And move on. Hatred and bitterness and regret are not part of God's plan for your life. Forgiveness is.

Our Savior kneels down and gazes upon the darkest acts of our lives. But rather than recoil in horror, he reaches out in kindness and says, "I can clean that if you want." And, from the basin of his grace, he scoops a palm full of mercy and washes our sin.

Max Lucado

A PRAYER FOR DADS

Lord, I know that I need to forgive others just as You have forgiven me. Help me to be an example of forgiveness to my children. Keep me mindful, Father, that I am never fully liberated until I have been freed from the chains of bitterness—and that You offer me that freedom through Your Son, Christ Jesus. Amen

What does the Bible say about enthusiasm?

THE QUICK ANSWER

Be enthusiastic about your faith: John Wesley wrote, "You don't have to advertise a fire. Get on fire for God and the world will come to watch you burn." When you allow yourself to become extremely enthusiastic about your faith, other people will notice—and so will God.

Enthused About Life

Whatever you do, do it enthusiastically,
as something done for the Lord and not for men.
Colossians 3:23 Holman CSB

Do you see each day as a glorious opportunity to serve God and to do His will? Are you enthused about life, or do you struggle through each day giving scarcely a thought to God's blessings? Are you constantly praising God for His gifts, and are you sharing His Good News with the world? And are you excited about the possibilities for service that God has placed before you, whether at home, at work, or at church? You should be.

You are the recipient of Christ's sacrificial love. Accept it enthusiastically and share it fervently. Jesus deserves your enthusiasm; the world deserves it; and you deserve the experience of sharing it.

When we wholeheartedly commit ourselves to God, there is nothing mediocre or run-of-the-mill about us. To live for Christ is to be passionate about our Lord and about our lives.

Jim Gallery

Wherever you are, be all there. Live to the hilt every situation you believe to be the will of God.

Jim Elliot

We act as though comfort and luxury were the chief requirements of life, when all we need to make us really happy is something to be enthusiastic about.

Charles Kingsley

A PRAYER FOR DADS

Dear Lord, You have called me not to a life of mediocrity, but to a life of passion. Today, I will be an enthusiastic follower of Your Son, and I will share His Good News—and His love—with all who cross my path. Amen

What does the Bible say about the power of faith?

THE QUICK ANSWER

Faith in God is contagious . . . and when it comes to your family's spiritual journey, no one's faith is more contagious than yours! Act, pray, praise, and trust God with the certain knowledge that your friends and family are watching . . . carefully!

When Mountains Need Moving

I assure you: If anyone says to this mountain, "Be lifted up and thrown into the sea," and does not doubt in his heart, but believes that what he says will happen, it will be done for him.
Mark 11:23 Holman CSB

Because we live in a demanding world, all of us have mountains to climb and mountains to move. Moving those mountains requires faith.

Are you a mountain-moving guy whose faith is evident for all to see? Or, are you a spiritual underachiever? As you think about the answer to that question, consider this: God needs more people who are willing to move mountains for His glory and for His kingdom.

Every life—including yours—is a series of wins and losses. Every step of the way, through every triumph and tragedy, God walks with you, ready and willing to strengthen you. So the next time you find your courage tested to the limit, remember to take your fears to God. If you call upon Him, you will be comforted. Whatever your challenge, whatever your trouble, God can handle it.

When you place your faith, your trust, indeed your life in the hands of your Heavenly Father, you'll be amazed at the marvelous things He can do with you and through you. So strengthen your faith through praise, through worship, through Bible study, and through prayer. And trust God's plans. With Him, all things are possible, and He stands ready to open a world of possibilities to you . . . if you have faith.

And now, with no more delays, let the mountain moving begin.

A PRAYER FOR DADS

Dear Lord, I want faith that moves mountains. You have big plans for this world and big plans for me. Help me fulfill those plans, Father, as I follow in the footsteps of Your Son. Amen

? QUESTION 45

What does the Bible say about the search for purpose and meaning?

THE QUICK ANSWER

God has a wonderful plan for you and your family. Discovering God's purpose requires a willingness to be open. God's plan is unfolding day by day. If you keep your eyes and your heart open, He'll reveal His plans. God has big things in store for you, but He may have quite a few lessons to teach you before you are fully prepared to do His will and fulfill His purposes.

The Search for Purpose

For everything, absolutely everything, above and below, visible and invisible, rank after rank after rank of angels—everything got started in him and finds its purpose in him.
Colossians 1:16 MSG

Life is best lived on purpose. And purpose, like everything else in the universe, begins with God. Whether you realize it or not, God has a plan for your life, a divine calling, a direction in which He is leading you. When you welcome God into your heart and establish a genuine relationship with Him, He will begin, in time, to make His purposes known.

Sometimes, God's intentions will be clear to you; other times, God's plan will seem uncertain at best. But even on those difficult days when you are unsure which way to turn, you must never lose sight of these overriding facts: God created you for a reason; He has important work for you to do; and He's waiting patiently for you to do it.

And the next step is up to you.

We must focus on prayer as the main thrust to accomplish God's will and purpose on earth. The forces against us have never been greater, and this is the only way we can release God's power to become victorious.

John Maxwell

When God speaks to you through the Bible, prayer, circumstances, the church, or in some other way, he has a purpose in mind for your life.

Henry Blackaby and Claude King

A PRAYER FOR DADS

Dear Lord, let Your purposes be my purposes. Let Your priorities be my priorities. Let Your will be my will. Let Your Word be my guide. And, let me grow in faith and in wisdom today and every day. Amen

? QUESTION 46

What does the Bible teach me about leadership, and about leading my family?

THE QUICK ANSWER

Since leadership comes in many forms, you can lead your family in your own way using your own style. Leadership is a responsibility that must not be taken lightly. If you choose to lead, you should first choose to follow Jesus.

The Need to Lead

Good leadership is a channel of water controlled by God;
he directs it to whatever ends he chooses.
Proverbs 21:1 MSG

As the leader of your family, you have a profound responsibility to your loved ones and to your God. If you desire to be an obedient servant to your Heavenly Father, you must lead your family according to His Holy Word. To do otherwise is to rob your loved ones of the peace and abundance that is rightfully theirs through the person of Jesus Christ.

Our world needs Christian leaders, and so does your family. So make this pledge and keep it: vow to become the godly leader that God intends you to be. Your family needs you, and you need the experience of leading them in the service of our Lord.

The test of a leader is taking the vision from me to we.

John Maxwell

What do we Christians chiefly value in our leaders? The answer seems to be not their holiness, but their gifts and skills and resources. The thought that only holy people are likely to be spiritually useful does not loom large in our minds.

J. I. Packer

Leaders must learn how to wait. Often their followers don't always see as far as they see or have the faith that they have.

Warren Wiersbe

A PRAYER FOR DADS

Dear Lord, when I find myself in a position of leadership, let me seek Your will and obey Your commandments. Make me a person of integrity and wisdom, Lord, and make me a worthy example to my family. Let me be a Christ-centered leader, and let me turn to You, Father, for guidance, for courage, for wisdom, and for love. Amen

God has given me special talents and unique opportunities. What should I do with my talents?

THE QUICK ANSWER

You, like every other person on earth, possess special abilities that can be nurtured carefully or ignored totally. The challenge, of course, is to do the former and to avoid the latter.

Using Your Gifts

I remind you to keep ablaze the gift of God that is in you.
2 Timothy 1:6 Holman CSB

Your talents are a gift from God. And, the same applies to your children. Their talents, too, are blessings from the Creator, blessings which must be nurtured or forfeited.

Are you and your loved ones willing to use your gifts in the way that God intends? Are you willing to summon the discipline that is required to develop your talents and to hone your skills? That's precisely what God wants you to do, and that's precisely what you should desire for yourself.

So be faithful stewards of your talents and treasures. And then prepare yourselves for even greater blessings that are sure to come.

God often reveals His direction for our lives through the way He made us . . . with a certain personality and unique skills.

Bill Hybels

You are the only person on earth who can use your ability.

Zig Ziglar

Employ whatever God has entrusted you with, in doing good, all possible good, in every possible kind and degree.

John Wesley

If you want to reach your potential, you need to add a strong work ethic to your talent.

John Maxwell

A PRAYER FOR DADS

Dear Lord, let me use my gifts, and let me help my children discover theirs. Your gifts are priceless and eternal—may we, as Your faithful children, use our own gifts to the glory of Your kingdom, today and forever. Amen

Sometimes I have trouble focusing my thoughts and energies. What does the Bible say about that?

THE QUICK ANSWER

The Lord wants you to focus your thoughts, your energies, your emotions, and your prayers on the things that really matter, and that means putting God first and family next.

Too Many Distractions?

Look straight ahead, and fix your eyes on what lies before you. Mark out a straight path for your feet; then stick to the path and stay safe. Don't get sidetracked; keep your feet from following evil.
Proverbs 4:25-27 NLT

All of us must live through those days when the traffic jams, the computer crashes, and the dog makes a main course out of our homework. But, when we find ourselves distracted by the minor frustrations of life, we must catch ourselves, take a deep breath, and lift our thoughts upward.

Although we may, at times, struggle mightily to rise above the distractions of everyday living, we need never struggle alone. God is here—eternal and faithful, with infinite patience and love—and, if we reach out to Him, He will restore our sense of perspective, He will give peace to our souls, and He will help us focus on the things that really matter.

As long as Jesus is one of many options, he is no option.

Max Lucado

Only the man who follows the command of Jesus single-mindedly and unresistingly let his yoke rest upon him, finds his burden easy, and under its gentle pressure receives the power to persevere in the right way.

Dietrich Bonhoeffer

Paul did one thing. Most of us dabble in forty things. Are you a doer or a dabbler?

Vance Havner

Give me the person who says, "This one thing I do, and not these fifty things I dabble in."

D. L. Moody

A PRAYER FOR DADS

Dear Lord, help me to face this day with a spirit of optimism and thanksgiving. And let me focus my thoughts on You and Your incomparable gifts. Amen

What does the Bible say about following my conscience?

THE QUICK ANSWER

That quiet little voice inside your head will guide you down the right path if you listen carefully. Very often, your conscience will actually tell you what God wants you to do. So listen, learn, and behave accordingly.

You and Your Conscience

If the way you live isn't consistent with what you believe,
then it's wrong.
Romans 14:23 MSG

Billy Graham correctly observed, "Most of us follow our conscience as we follow a wheelbarrow. We push it in front of us in the direction we want to go." To do so, of course, is a profound mistake. Yet all of us, on occasion, have failed to listen to the voice that God planted in our hearts, and all of us have suffered the consequences.

God gave you a conscience for a very good reason: to make your path conform to His will. Wise believers make it a practice to listen carefully to that quiet internal voice. Count yourself among that number. When your conscience speaks, listen and learn. In all likelihood, God is trying to get His message through. And in all likelihood, it is a message that you desperately need to hear.

To go against one's conscience is neither safe nor right. Here I stand. I cannot do otherwise.

Martin Luther

The convicting work of the Holy Spirit awakens, disturbs, and judges.

Franklin Graham

The beginning of backsliding means your conscience does not answer to the truth.

Oswald Sanders

A good conscience is a continual feast.

Francis Bacon

A PRAYER FOR DADS

Dear Lord, You speak to me through the gift of Your Holy Word. And, Father, You speak to me through that still small voice that tells me right from wrong. Let me follow Your way, Lord, and, in these quiet moments, show me Your plan for this day, that I might serve You. Amen

?QUESTION 50

What does the Bible say about God's love?

THE QUICK ANSWER

When all else fails, God's love does not. You can always depend upon God's love . . . and He is always your ultimate protection.

Embracing God's Love

Unfailing love surrounds those who trust the LORD.
Psalm 32:10 NLT

As Christian dads who have been saved by God's grace, we have a profound responsibility to educate our children in the ways of the Lord. God is a loving Father. We are God's children, and we are called upon to be faithful to Him.

When we embrace God's love, we are forever changed. When we embrace God's love, we feel differently about our neighbors, our world, and ourselves. When we embrace God's love, we tell and retell the wondrous story of His Son.

We return our Father's love by sharing it with others. We honor our Heavenly Father by obeying His commandments and sharing His Good News. When we do, we are blessed . . . and the Father smiles.

If you have an obedience problem, you have a love problem. Focus your attention on God's love.

Henry Blackaby

Even when we cannot see the why and wherefore of God's dealings, we know that there is love in and behind them, so we can rejoice always.

J. I. Packer

The life of faith is a daily exploration of the constant and countless ways in which God's grace and love are experienced.

Eugene Peterson

God has pursued us from farther than space and longer than time.

John Eldredge

A PRAYER FOR DADS

Thank You, Dear God, for Your love. You are my loving Father. I thank You for Your love and for Your Son. I will praise You; I will worship You; and, I will love You today, tomorrow, and forever. Amen

? QUESTION 51

Sometimes, I am afraid. What does the Bible say about fear?

THE QUICK ANSWER

If you're feeling fearful or anxious, you must trust God to solve the problems that are simply too big for you to solve.

Beyond Fear

I sought the Lord, and He answered me
and delivered me from all my fears.
Psalm 34:4 Holman CSB

We live in a world that is, at times, a frightening place. We live in a world that is, at times, a discouraging place. We live in a world where life-changing losses can be so painful and so profound that it seems we will never recover. But, with God's help, and with the help of encouraging family members and friends, we can recover.

During the darker days of life, we are wise to remember the words of Jesus, who reassured His disciples, saying, "Take courage! It is I. Don't be afraid" (Matthew 14:27 NIV). Then, with God's comfort and His love in our hearts, we can offer encouragement to others. And by helping them face their fears, we can, in turn, tackle our own problems with courage, determination, and faith.

———————————————

When we meditate on God and remember the promises He has given us in His Word, our faith grows, and our fears dissolve.

Charles Stanley

One of the main missions of God is to free us from the debilitating bonds of fear and anxiety. God's heart is broken when He sees us so demoralized and weighed down by fear.

Bill Hybels

When we submit difficult and alarming situations to God, he promises that his peace will be like a military garrison to guard our hearts from fear.

Dennis Swanberg

A PRAYER FOR DADS

Your Word reminds me, Lord, that even when I walk through the valley of the shadow of death, I need fear no evil, for You are with me, and You comfort me. Thank You, Lord, for a perfect love that casts out fear. Let me live courageously and faithfully this day and every day. Amen

There's so much to learn. How can my family and I keep up with it all?

THE QUICK ANSWER

Simple: you've got to keep learning and growing every day. And remember the advice of centenarian Marie T. Freeman: "Stay interested in everything and everybody. It keeps you young."

Lifetime Learning

Start with God—the first step in learning is bowing down to God.
Proverbs 1:7 MSG

Whether you're twenty-two or a hundred and two, you've still got lots to learn. Even if you're a very wise man, God isn't finished with you yet, and He isn't finished teaching you important lessons about life here on earth and life eternal.

Do you seek to live a life of righteousness and wisdom? If so, you must continue to study the ultimate source of wisdom: the Word of God. You must associate, day in and day out, with godly men and women. And, you must act in accordance with your beliefs. When you study God's Word and live according to His commandments, you will become wise . . . and you will be a blessing to your friends, to your family, and to the world.

The wonderful thing about God's schoolroom is that we get to grade our own papers. You see, He doesn't test us so He can learn how well we're doing. He tests us so we can discover how well we're doing.

Charles Swindoll

Knowledge is power.

Francis Bacon

The wise man gives proper appreciation in his life to his past. He learns to sift the sawdust of heritage in order to find the nuggets that make the current moment have any meaning.

Grady Nutt

It's the things you learn after you know it all that really count.

Vance Havner

A PRAYER FOR DADS

Dear Lord, I have so much to learn. Help me to watch, to listen, to think, and to learn, every day of my life. Amen

Everybody (including me) has problems. What can God's Word teach me about my problems?

THE QUICK ANSWER

When it comes to solving problems, work beats worry. Remember: It is better to fix than to fret.

Problem-solving 101

People who do what is right may have many problems,
but the Lord will solve them all.
Psalm 34:19 NCV

Life is an adventure in problem-solving. The question is not whether we will encounter problems; the real question is how we will choose to address them. When it comes to solving the problems of everyday living, we often know precisely what needs to be done, but we may be slow in doing it—especially if what needs to be done is difficult. So we put off till tomorrow what should be done today.

As a man living here in the 21st century, you have your own set of challenges. As you face those challenges, you may be comforted by this fact: Trouble, of every kind, is temporary. Yet God's grace is eternal. And worries, of every kind, are temporary. But God's love is everlasting. The troubles that concern you will pass. God remains. And for every problem, God has a solution.

The words of Psalm 34 remind us that the Lord solves problems for "people who do what is right." And usually, doing "what is right" means doing the uncomfortable work of confronting our problems sooner rather than later. So with no further ado, let the problem-solving begin . . . right now.

We are all faced with a series of great opportunities, brilliantly disguised as unsolvable problems. Unsolvable without God's wisdom, that is.

Charles Swindoll

Life will be made or broken at the place where we meet and deal with obstacles.

E. Stanley Jones

A PRAYER FOR DADS

Lord, sometimes my problems are simply too big for me, but they are never too big for You. Let me turn my troubles over to You, Lord, and let me trust in You today and for all eternity. Amen

Sometimes, I can be overly critical of my family members. What does the Bible say about that?

THE QUICK ANSWER

If you're tempted to be critical of others, remember that you must treat others in the way you want to be treated. So do everybody (including yourself) a favor: don't be overly critical. And husbands beware: You cannot pursue intimacy with God while demeaning your wife. So you must never, never, never demean your wife for any reason. Never.

Critics Beware

Don't criticize one another, brothers. He who criticizes a brother or judges his brother criticizes the law and judges the law. But if you judge the law, you are not a doer of the law but a judge.
James 4:11 Holman CSB

From experience, we know that it is easier to criticize than to correct; we understand that it is easier to find faults than solutions; and we realize that excessive criticism is usually destructive, not productive. Yet the urge to criticize others remains a powerful temptation for most of us. Our task, as obedient believers, is to break the twin habits of negative thinking and critical speech.

Negativity is highly contagious: we give it to others who, in turn, give it back to us. This cycle can be broken by positive thoughts, heartfelt prayers, and encouraging words. As thoughtful servants of a loving God, we can use the transforming power of Christ's love to break the chains of negativity. And we should.

The scrutiny we give other people should be for ourselves.

Oswald Chambers

We shall never come to the perfect man til we come to the perfect world.

Matthew Henry

After one hour in heaven, we shall be ashamed that we ever grumbled.

Vance Havner

A PRAYER FOR DADS

Help me, Lord, rise above the need to criticize others. May my own shortcomings humble me, and may I always be a source of genuine encouragement to my family and friends. Amen

QUESTION 55

What's the best way for me to communicate my beliefs to my loved ones?

THE QUICK ANSWER

By your words and your example. And the greatest of these is example.

Your Beliefs

Do what God's teaching says; when you only listen and do nothing, you are fooling yourselves.
James 1:22 NCV

In describing one's beliefs, actions are far better descriptors than words. Yet far too many of us spend more energy talking about our beliefs than living by them—with predictable consequences.

Is your life a picture book of your creed? Are your actions congruent with your beliefs? Are you willing to practice the philosophy that you preach?

Today and every day, make certain that your actions are guided by God's Word and by the conscience that He has placed in your heart. Don't treat your faith as if it were separate from your everyday life. Weave your beliefs into the very fabric of your day. When you do, God will honor your good works, and your good works will honor God.

Once you have thoroughly examined your values and articulated them, you will be able to steer your life by them.

John Maxwell

Believe and do what God says. The life-changing consequences will be limitless, and the results will be confidence and peace of mind.

Franklin Graham

God calls us to be committed to Him, to be committed to making a difference, and to be committed to reconciliation.

Bill Hybels

The reason many of us do not ardently believe in the gospel is that we have never given it a rigorous testing, thrown our hard questions at it, or faced it with our most prickly doubts.

Eugene Peterson

A PRAYER FOR DADS

Heavenly Father, I believe in You, and I believe in Your Word. Help me to live in such a way that my actions validate my beliefs—and let the glory be Yours forever. Amen

What does the Bible say about fearing God?

THE QUICK ANSWER

It's simple: If you have a healthy fear of God, you're wise—if you don't, you're not.

The Right Kind of Fear

A simple life in the Fear-of-God is better than a rich life with a ton of headaches.

Proverbs 15:16 MSG

God's hand shapes the universe, and it shapes our lives. God maintains absolute sovereignty over His creation, and His power is beyond comprehension. As believers, we must cultivate a sincere respect for God's awesome power. God has dominion over all things, and until we acknowledge His sovereignty, we lack the humility we need to live righteously, and we lack the humility we need to become wise.

The fear of the Lord is, indeed, the beginning of knowledge. So today, as you face the realities of everyday life, remember this: until you acquire a healthy, respectful fear of God's power, your education is incomplete, and so is your faith.

The remarkable thing about fearing God is that when you fear God, you fear nothing else, whereas if you do not fear God, you fear everything else.

Oswald Chambers

When true believers are awed by the greatness of God and by the privilege of becoming His children, then they become sincerely motivated, effective evangelists.

Bill Hybels

A healthy fear of God will do much to deter us from sin.

Charles Swindoll

The fear of God is the death of every other fear.

C. H. Spurgeon

A PRAYER FOR DADS

Lord, You love me and protect me. I praise You, Father, for Your grace, and I respect You for Your infinite power. Let my greatest fear in life be the fear of displeasing You. Amen

QUESTION 57

What does the Bible have to say about the importance of rejoicing?

THE QUICK ANSWER

It's important to rejoice and praise the Father. Joy begins with a choice—the choice to establish a genuine relationship with God and His Son. Joy does not depend upon your circumstances, but upon your relationship with God.

Rejoice Now!

O clap your hands, all peoples; Shout to God with the voice of joy.
Psalm 47:1 NASB

Have you made the choice to rejoice? Hopefully so. After all, if you're a believer, you have plenty of reasons to be joyful. Yet sometimes, amid the inevitable hustle and bustle of life, you may lose sight of your blessings as you wrestle with the challenges of everyday life.

Christ made it clear to His followers: He intended that His joy would become their joy. And it still holds true today: Christ intends that His believers share His love with His joy in their hearts.

What does life have in store for you? A world full of possibilities (of course it's up to you to seize them) and God's promise of abundance (of course it's up to you to accept it). So, as you embark upon the next phase of your journey, remember to celebrate the life that God has given you. Your Creator has blessed you beyond measure. Honor Him with your prayers, your words, your deeds, and your joy.

Joy is the serious business of heaven.

C. S. Lewis

As Catherine of Siena said, "All the way to heaven is heaven." A joyful end requires a joyful means. Bless the Lord.

Eugene Peterson

Some of us seem so anxious about avoiding hell that we forget to celebrate our journey toward heaven.

Philip Yancey

A PRAYER FOR DADS

Dear Lord, You have given me so many blessings; let me celebrate Your gifts. Make me thankful, loving, responsible, and wise. I praise You, Father, for the gift of Your Son and for the priceless gift of salvation. Make me be a joyful Christian and a worthy example to my loved ones, today and every day. Amen

?QUESTION 58

The Bible says I should imitate Christ, but I can never be like Him. So what should I do?

THE QUICK ANSWER

While you can't imitate Christ perfectly, you can follow in His footsteps, you can share His Good News, and you can, to the best of your abilities, obey His commandments. And that's what you should do.

Imitating the Master

Therefore, be imitators of God, as dearly loved children.
Ephesians 5:1 Holman CSB

Imitating Christ is impossible, but attempting to imitate Him is both possible and advisable. By attempting to imitate Jesus, we seek, to the best of our abilities, to walk in His footsteps. To the extent we succeed in following Him, we receive the spiritual abundance that is the rightful possession of those who love Christ and keep His commandments.

Do you seek God's blessings for the day ahead? Then, to the best of your abilities, imitate His Son. You will fall short, of course. But if your heart is right and your intentions are pure, God will bless your efforts, your day, and your life.

Christlikeness is not produced by imitation, but by inhabitation.

Rick Warren

Every Christian is to become a little Christ. The whole purpose of becoming a Christian is simply nothing else.

C. S. Lewis

Lord, I am no longer my own, but Yours. Put me to what You will, rank me with whom You will. Let me be employed by You or laid aside for You, exalted for You or brought low by You. Let me have all things, let me have nothing. I freely and heartily yield all things to Your pleasure and disposal. And now, O glorious and blessed God, Father, Son, and Holy Spirit, You are mine and I am Yours. So be it. Amen.

John Wesley

A PRAYER FOR DADS

Dear Jesus, because I am Your disciple, I will trust You, I will obey Your teachings, and I will share Your Good News. You have given me life abundant and life eternal, and I will follow You today and forever. Amen

I want to sense a calling from God. What does the Bible say about that?

THE QUICK ANSWER

If you ask God for His guidance, He will give it (John 10:10). And then, when you sense God's leading, your responsibility is clear: to answer His call.

Answering the Call

God chose you to be his people, so I urge you now to live the life to which God called you.
Ephesians 4:1 NCV

It is vitally important that you heed God's call. In John 15:16, Jesus says, "You did not choose me, but I chose you and appointed you to go and bear fruit—fruit that will last" (NIV). In other words, you have been called by Christ, and now, it is up to you to decide precisely how you will answer.

Have you already found your special calling? If so, you're a very lucky guy. If not, keep searching and keep praying until you discover it. And remember this: God has important work for you to do—work that no one else on earth can accomplish but you.

The world does not consider labor a blessing, therefore it flees and hates it, but the pious who fear the Lord labor with a ready and cheerful heart, for they know God's command, and they acknowledge His calling.

Martin Luther

When you become consumed by God's call on your life, everything will take on new meaning and significance. You will begin to see every facet of your life, including your pain, as a means through which God can work to bring others to Himself.

Charles Stanley

God never calls without enabling us. In other words, if he calls you to do something, he makes it possible for you to do it.

Luci Swindoll

A PRAYER FOR DADS

Heavenly Father, You have called me, and I acknowledge that calling. In these quiet moments before this busy day unfolds, I come to You. I will study Your Word and seek Your guidance. Give me the wisdom to know Your will for my life and the courage to follow wherever You may lead me, today and forever. Amen

The Bible makes many promises. Can I depend upon those promises?

THE QUICK ANSWER

Yes! God is always faithful and His Word endures forever. So you and your family should study God's Word (every day) and trust it. When you do, you will be blessed.

He Keeps His Promises

Let us hold on to the confession of our hope without wavering, for He who promised is faithful.
Hebrews 10:23 Holman CSB

God has made quite a few promises to you, and He intends to keep every single one of them. You will find these promises in a book like no other: the Holy Bible. The Bible is your roadmap for life here on earth and for life eternal—as a believer, you are called upon to trust its promises, to follow its commandments, and to share its Good News.

God has made promises to all of humanity and to you. God's promises never fail and they never grow old. You must trust those promises and share them with your family, with your friends, and with the world . . . starting now . . . and ending never.

There are four words I wish we would never forget, and they are, "God keeps his word."

Charles Swindoll

The stars may fall, but God's promises will stand and be fulfilled.

J. I. Packer

God's promises are overflowings from his great heart.

C. H. Spurgeon

The promises of Scripture are not mere pious hopes or sanctified guesses. They are more than sentimental words to be printed on decorated cards for Sunday School children. They are eternal verities. They are true. There is no perhaps about them.

Peter Marshall

A PRAYER FOR DADS

Lord, Your Holy Word contains promises, and I will trust them. I will use the Bible as my guide, and I will trust You, Lord, to speak to me through Your Holy Spirit and through Your Holy Word, this day and forever. Amen

QUESTION 61

What does the Bible say about eternal life?

THE QUICK ANSWER

God offers you a priceless gift: the gift of eternal life. If you have not already done so, accept God's gift today—tomorrow may be too late.

The Gift of Eternal Life

Just then someone came up and asked Him,
"Teacher, what good must I do to have eternal life?"
"Why do you ask Me about what is good?" He said to him.
"There is only One who is good. If you want to enter into life,
keep the commandments."
Matthew 19:16-17 Holman CSB

Your ability to envision the future, like your life here on earth, is limited. God's vision, however, is not burdened by any such limitations. He sees all things, He knows all things, and His plans for you extend throughout eternity.

God's plans are not limited to the events of daily life. Your Heavenly Father has bigger things in mind for you . . . much bigger things. So praise the Creator for the gift of eternal life and share the Good News with all who cross your path. And remember: if you have given your heart to the Son, you belong to the Father—today, tomorrow, and for all eternity.

Someday you will read in the papers that Moody is dead. Don't you believe a word of it. At that moment I shall be more alive than I am now. I was born of the flesh in 1837, I was born of the spirit in 1855. That which is born of the flesh may die. That which is born of the Spirit shall live forever.

D. L. Moody

God loves you and wants you to experience peace and life—abundant and eternal.

Billy Graham

Once a man is united to God, how could he not live forever? Once a man is separated from God, what can he do but wither and die?

C. S. Lewis

A PRAYER FOR DADS

Lord, I am only here on this earth for a brief while. But, You have offered me the priceless gift of eternal life through Your Son Jesus. I accept Your gift, Lord, with thanksgiving and praise. Let me share the good news of my salvation with those who need Your healing touch. Amen

Sundays have become very busy around our house. Our schedules are full, and we hardly have time to slow down long enough to catch our breath. In the future, how should we reorganize our Sundays?

THE QUICK ANSWER

The world considers Sunday to be just another day—but you shouldn't fall prey to that sort of thinking. As a Christian parent, it's up to you to decide how your family will spend Sundays. Please decide wisely.

Observing the Sabbath

Remember the Sabbath day, to keep it holy.
Exodus 20:8 NKJV

When God gave Moses the Ten Commandments, it became perfectly clear that our Heavenly Father intends for us to make the Sabbath a holy day, a day for worship, for contemplation, for fellowship, and for rest. Yet we live in a seven-day-a-week world, a world that all too often treats Sunday as a regular workday.

How does your family observe the Lord's day? When church is over, do you treat Sunday like any other day of the week? If so, it's time to think long and hard about your family's schedule and your family's priorities.

Whenever we ignore God's commandments, we pay a price. So if you've been treating Sunday as just another day, it's time to break that habit. When Sunday rolls around, don't try to fill every spare moment. Take time to rest . . . Father's orders!

———————————————

Worship is not taught from the pulpit. It must be learned in the heart.

Jim Elliot

Worship is a daunting task. Each worships differently. But each should worship.

Max Lucado

God has promised to give you all of eternity. The least you can do is give Him one day a week in return.

Marie T. Freeman

A PRAYER FOR DADS

Dear Lord, I thank You for the Sabbath day, a day when my family and I can worship You and praise Your Son. We will keep the Sabbath as a holy day, a day when we can honor You. Amen

How does the Bible instruct me to direct my thoughts?

THE QUICK ANSWER

Watch what you think: If your inner voice is, in reality, your inner critic, you need to tone down the criticism now. And while you're at it, train yourself to begin thinking thoughts that are more rational, more accepting, and less judgmental.

The Direction of Your Thoughts

Fix your thoughts on what is true and honorable and right.
Think about things that are pure and lovely and admirable.
Think about things that are excellent and worthy of praise.
Philippians 4:8 NLT

Thoughts are intensely powerful things. Our thoughts have the power to lift us up or drag us down; they have the power to energize us or deplete us, to inspire us to greater accomplishments or to make those accomplishments impossible.

How will you and your family members direct your thoughts today? Will you obey the words of Philippians 4:8 by dwelling upon those things that are honorable, true, and worthy of praise? Or will you allow your thoughts to be hijacked by the negativity that seems to dominate our troubled world?

Are you fearful, angry, bored, or worried? Are you so preoccupied with the concerns of this day that you fail to thank God for the promise of eternity? Are you confused, bitter, or pessimistic? If so, God wants to have a little talk with you.

God intends that you experience joy and abundance, but He will not force His joy upon you; you must claim it for yourself. It's up to you and your loved ones to celebrate the life that God has given you by focusing your minds upon "whatever is commendable." So form the habit of spending more time thinking about your blessings and less time fretting about your hardships. Then, take time to thank the Giver of all things good for gifts that are, in truth, far too numerous to count.

A PRAYER FOR DADS

Dear Lord, I will focus on Your love, Your power, Your promises, and Your Son. When I am weak, I will turn to You for strength; when I am worried, I will turn to You for comfort; when I am troubled, I will turn to You for patience and perspective. Help me guard my thoughts, Lord, so that I may honor You this day and forever. Amen

? QUESTION 64

Sometimes I'm impatient for life to unfold. What does the Bible say about God's timing?

THE QUICK ANSWER

God has very big plans in store for your life, so trust Him and wait patiently for those plans to unfold. And remember: God's timing is best, so don't allow yourself to become discouraged if things don't work out exactly as you wish. Instead of worrying about your future, entrust it to God. He knows exactly what you need and exactly when you need it.

God's Timetable

He has made everything beautiful in its time.
He has also set eternity in the hearts of men;
yet they cannot fathom what God has done from beginning to end.
Ecclesiastes 3:11 NIV

Are you anxious for God to work out His plan for your life? Who isn't? As believers, we all want God to do great things for us and through us, and we want Him to do those things now. But sometimes, God has other plans. Sometimes, God's timetable does not coincide with our own. It's worth noting, however, that God's timetable is always perfect.

The next time you find your patience tested to the limit, remember that the world unfolds according to God's plan, not ours. Sometimes, we must wait patiently, and that's as it should be. After all, think how patient God has been with us.

God has a designated time when his promise will be fulfilled and the prayer will be answered.

Jim Cymbala

God is in no hurry. Compared to the works of mankind, He is extremely deliberate. God is not a slave to the human clock.

Charles Swindoll

The stops of a good man are ordered by the Lord as well as his steps.

George Mueller

A PRAYER FOR DADS

Dear Lord, Your wisdom is infinite, and the timing of Your heavenly plan is perfect. You have a plan for my life that is grander than I can imagine. When I am impatient, remind me that You are never early or late. You are always on time, Father, so let me trust in You. Amen

? QUESTION 65

What does the Bible say about discipleship?

THE QUICK ANSWER

God's Word instructs you to follow in Christ's footsteps. And when it comes to discipleship, you owe it, not just to yourself or to God, but also to your family to be a devoted follower of the One from Galilee.

The Decision to Be His Disciple

He has showed you, O man, what is good.
And what does the LORD require of you? To act justly
and to love mercy and to walk humbly with your God.
Micah 6:8 NIV

When Jesus addressed His disciples, He warned that each one must, "take up his cross and follow me." The disciples must have known exactly what the Master meant. In Jesus' day, prisoners were forced to carry their own crosses to the location where they would be put to death. Thus, Christ's message was clear: in order to follow Him, Christ's disciples must deny themselves and, instead, trust Him completely. Nothing has changed since then.

If we are to be disciples of Christ, we must trust Him and place Him at the very center of our beings. Jesus never comes "next." He is always first. The paradox, of course, is that only by sacrificing ourselves to Him do we gain salvation for ourselves.

Do you seek to be a worthy disciple of Christ? Then pick up His cross today and every day that you live. When you do, He will bless you now and forever.

As we seek to become disciples of Jesus Christ, we should never forget that the word *disciple* is directly related to the word *discipline*. To be a disciple of the Lord Jesus Christ is to know his discipline.

Dennis Swanberg

It is the secret of true discipleship to bear the cross, to acknowledge the death sentence that has been passed on self, and to deny any right that self has to rule over us.

Andrew Murray

A PRAYER FOR DADS

Help me, Lord, to understand what cross I am to bear this day. Give me the strength and the courage to carry that cross along the path of Your choosing so that I may be a worthy disciple of Your Son. Amen

We live in a noisy world where it's hard to find a moment's peace. What does the Bible teach us about peace?

THE QUICK ANSWER

God's peace surpasses human understanding. When you accept His peace, it will revolutionize your life.

Accepting His Peace

And the peace of God, which surpasses all comprehension,
will guard your hearts and your minds in Christ Jesus.
Philippians 4:7 NASB

As a busy father, your plate is probably full: kids to care for, bills to pay, a family to lead. Sometimes it seems that you can scarcely find a moment's peace. But the beautiful words of John 14:27 are a reminder that God's peace is always available to you.

Jesus said, "Peace I leave with you, my peace I give unto you . . . ." Christ offers us peace, not as the world gives, but as He alone gives. We, as believers, can accept His peace or ignore it.

When we accept the peace of Jesus Christ into our hearts, our lives are transformed. And then, because we possess the gift of peace, we can share that gift with fellow Christians, family members, friends, and associates. If, on the other hand, we choose to ignore the gift of peace—for whatever reason—we simply cannot share what we do not possess.

Today, as a gift to yourself, to your family, and to your friends, claim the inner peace that is your spiritual birthright: the peace of Jesus Christ. It is offered freely; it has been paid for in full; it is yours for the asking. So ask. And then share.

A great many people are trying to make peace, but that has already been done. God has not left it for us to do; all we have to do is to enter into it.

D. L. Moody

The Bible instructs—and experience teaches—that praising God results in our burdens being lifted and our joys being multiplied.

Jim Gallery

A PRAYER FOR DADS

Dear Lord, the peace that the world offers is fleeting, but You offer a peace that is perfect and eternal. Let me take my concerns and burdens to You, Father, and let me feel the spiritual abundance that You offer through the person of Your Son, the Prince of Peace. Amen

QUESTION 67

I want to sense God's presence. What should I do?

THE QUICK ANSWER

God isn't far away—He's right here, right now. And He's willing to talk to you right here, right now. So find a quiet place and open your heart to Him. When you do, you'll sense God's presence and His love, which, by the way, is already surrounding you and your loved ones.

He's Here

I am not alone, because the Father is with Me.
John 16:32 Holman CSB

Where is God? God is eternally with us. He is omnipresent. He is, quite literally, everywhere you have ever been and everywhere you will ever go. He is with you night and day; He knows your every thought; He hears your every heartbeat.

Sometimes, in the crush of your daily duties, God may seem far away. Or sometimes, when the disappointments and sorrows of life leave you brokenhearted, God may seem distant, but He is not. When you earnestly seek God, you will find Him because He is here, waiting patiently for you to reach out to Him . . . right here . . . right now.

There is a basic urge: the longing for unity. You desire a reunion with God—with God your Father.

E. Stanley Jones

The next time you hear a baby laugh or see an ocean wave, take note. Pause and listen as his Majesty whispers ever so gently, "I'm here."

Max Lucado

Get yourself into the presence of the loving Father. Just place yourself before Him, and look up into, His face; think of His love, His wonderful, tender, pitying love.

Andrew Murray

God is at work; He is in full control; He is in the midst of whatever has happened, is happening, and will happen.

Charles Swindoll

A PRAYER FOR DADS

Dear Lord, You are with me always. Help me feel Your presence in every situation and every circumstance. Today, Dear God, let me feel You and acknowledge Your presence, Your love, and Your Son. Amen

I learned the Golden Rule as a child, but now that I'm an adult, what should it mean to me?

THE QUICK ANSWER

The Golden Rule applies to all believers of all ages, including you. That means that you must strive to treat other people—all people—in the same way you want to be treated. No exceptions.

His Golden Rule

Do to others as you would have them do to you.
Luke 6:31 NIV

Some rules are easier to understand than they are to live by. Jesus told us that we should treat other people in the same way that we want to be treated: that's the Golden Rule. But sometimes, especially when we're feeling pressure from friends, or when we're tired or upset, obeying the Golden Rule can seem like an impossible task—but it's not.

God wants us to treat other people with respect, kindness, and courtesy. He wants us to rise above our own imperfections, and He wants us to treat others with unselfishness and love. To make it sort and sweet, God wants us to obey the Golden Rule, and He knows we can do it.

So if you're wondering how to treat someone else, ask the person you see every time you look into the mirror. The answer you receive will tell you exactly what to do.

The mark of a Christian is that he will walk the second mile and turn the other cheek. A wise man or woman gives the extra effort, all for the glory of the Lord Jesus Christ.

John Maxwell

When you extend hospitality to others, you're not trying to impress people, you're trying to reflect God to them.

Max Lucado

It is one of the most beautiful compensations of life that no one can sincerely try to help another without helping herself.

Barbara Johnson

A PRAYER FOR DADS

Dear Lord, the Golden Rule is not only a perfect standard to use with my friends and neighbors; it is also a guide for raising my children. Enable me to respect my children as I want them to respect me. Help me to walk in their shoes and to see life from their perspective. Help me, Father, to be a nurturing, loving parent every day that I live, and may the glory be yours. Amen

What does God's Word say about God's Son?

THE QUICK ANSWER

What a friend you have in Jesus: Jesus loves you, and He offers you eternal life with Him in heaven. Welcome Him into your heart. Now!

What a Friend

Therefore if any man be in Christ, he is a new creature:
old things are passed away; behold, all things are become new.
2 Corinthians 5:17 KJV

Our circumstances change but Jesus does not. Even when the world seems to be trembling beneath our feet, Jesus remains the spiritual bedrock that cannot be moved.

The old familiar hymn begins, "What a friend we have in Jesus . . . ." No truer words were ever penned. Jesus is the sovereign Friend and ultimate Savior of mankind. Christ showed enduring love for His believers by willingly sacrificing His own life so that we might have eternal life. Let us love Him, praise Him, and share His message of salvation with our neighbors and with the world.

Jesus came into the world so we could know, once and for all, that God is concerned about the way we live, the way we believe, and the way we die.

Billy Graham

Jesus: the proof of God's love.

Philip Yancey

Jesus was the perfect reflection of God's nature in every situation He encountered during His time here on earth.

Bill Hybels

Jesus is the personal approach from the unseen God coming so near that he becomes inescapable. You don't have to find him you just have to consent to be found.

E. Stanley Jones

A PRAYER FOR DADS

Heavenly Father, I praise You for Your Son. Jesus is my Savior and my strength. Let me share His Good News with all who cross my path, and let me share His love with all who need His healing touch. Amen

? QUESTION 70

Sometimes it's hard to be an obedient Christian. What does the Bible say about obedience?

THE QUICK ANSWER

God rewards obedience and punishes disobedience. It's not enough to understand God's rules; you must also live by them or face the consequences.

Obedience Now

Not everyone who says to Me, "Lord, Lord!" will enter the kingdom of heaven, but the one who does the will of My Father in heaven.
Matthew 7:21 Holman CSB

God's laws are eternal and unchanging: obedience leads to abundance and joy; disobedience leads to disaster. God has given us a guidebook for righteous living called the Holy Bible. If we trust God's Word and live by it, we are blessed. But, if we choose to ignore God's commandments, the results are as predictable as they are tragic.

Life is a series of decisions and choices. Each day, we make countless decisions that can bring us closer to God . . . or not. When we live according to God's commandments, we earn for ourselves the abundance and peace that He intends for our lives.

Do you seek God's peace and His blessings? Then obey Him. When you're faced with a difficult choice or a powerful temptation, seek God's counsel and trust the counsel He gives. Invite God into your heart and live according to His commandments. When you do, you will be blessed today and tomorrow and forever.

Believe and do what God says. The life-changing consequences will be limitless, and the results will be confidence and peace of mind.

Franklin Graham

Trials and sufferings teach us to obey the Lord by faith, and we soon learn that obedience pays off in joyful ways.

Bill Bright

A PRAYER FOR DADS

Lord, my family is both a priceless gift and a profound responsibility. Let my actions be worthy of that responsibility. Lead me along Your path, Lord, and guide me far from the frustrations and distractions of this troubled world. Let Your Holy Word guide my actions, and let Your love reside in my heart, this day and every day. Amen

? QUESTION 71

What does the Bible say about family life?

THE QUICK ANSWER

Your family is God's gift to you. And as a parent, you have profound responsibilities: To build your family on the firm foundation of God's love, to teach your children the wisdom of God's Word, and to serve as a positive role model to family, to friends, and to the world.

Caring for Your Family

Whoever does not care for his own relatives, especially his own family members, has turned against the faith and is worse than someone who does not believe in God.

1 Timothy 5:8 NCV

The words of 1 Timothy 5:8 are unambiguous: if God has blessed us with families, then He expects us to care for them. Sometimes, this profound responsibility seems daunting. And sometimes, even for the most dedicated Christian men, family life holds moments of frustration and disappointment. But, for those who are lucky enough to live in the presence of a close-knit, caring clan, the rewards far outweigh the demands.

No family is perfect, and neither is yours. Despite the inevitable challenges of providing for your family, and despite the occasional hurt feelings of family life, your clan is God's gift to you. Give thanks to the Giver for the gift of family . . . and act accordingly.

It is a reverent thing to see an ancient castle or building not in decay, or to see a fair timber tree sound and perfect. How much more beautiful it is to behold an ancient and noble family that has stood against the waves and weathers of time.

Francis Bacon

Never give your family the leftovers and crumbs of your time.

Charles Swindoll

The only true source of meaning in life is found in love for God and his son Jesus Christ, and love for mankind, beginning with our own families.

James Dobson

A PRAYER FOR DADS

Lord, You have given me a family to love and to care for. Thank You, Father. I will love all the members of my family despite their imperfections. Let them love me, Dear Lord, despite mine. Amen

QUESTION 72

Sometimes it's hard to be hopeful. What does the Bible say about hope?

THE QUICK ANSWER

Don't give up hope: Other people have experienced the same kind of hard times you may be experiencing now. They made it, and so can you (Psalm 146:5).

Finding Hope

This hope we have as an anchor of the soul,
a hope both sure and steadfast.
Hebrews 6:19 NASB

Are you a hope-filled father? You should be. After all, God is good; His love endures; and He has offered you the priceless gift of eternal life.

But sometimes hope slips away, even for the most optimistic pops. Despite God's promises, despite Christ's love, and despite our countless blessings, we can still fall prey to discouragement and doubt. When we do, we need the encouragement of fellow believers, the life-changing power of prayer, and the healing truth of God's Holy Word.

If you find yourself falling into the spiritual traps of worry and discouragement, seek the healing touch of Jesus and the encouraging words of fellow Christians. If you find a friend in need, remind him or her of the peace that is found through a personal relationship with Christ. This world can be a place of trials and tribulations, but as believers, we are secure. God has promised us peace, joy, and eternal life. And, of course, God keeps His promises today, tomorrow, and forever.

Faith looks back and draws courage; hope looks ahead and keeps desire alive.

John Eldredge

If your hopes are being disappointed just now, it means that they are being purified.

Oswald Chambers

The hope we have in Jesus is the anchor for the soul—something sure and steadfast, preventing drifting or giving way, lowered to the depth of God's love.

Franklin Graham

A PRAYER FOR DADS

Today, Dear Lord, I will live in hope. If I become discouraged, I will turn to You. If I grow weary, I will seek strength in You. In every aspect of my life, I will trust You. You are my Father, Lord, and I place my hope and my faith in You. Amen

I would like to believe that I am protected by God. What does the Bible say about that?

THE QUICK ANSWER

You are protected by God . . . now and always. Earthly security is an illusion. Your only real security comes from the loving heart of God.

The Ultimate Armor

If God is for us, who is against us?
Romans 8:31 Holman CSB

God has promised to protect us, and He intends to keep His promise. In a world filled with dangers and temptations, God is the ultimate armor. In a world filled with misleading messages, God's Word is the ultimate truth. In a world filled with more frustrations than we can count, God's Son offers the ultimate peace.

Will you accept God's peace and wear God's armor against the dangers of our world? Hopefully so—because when you do, you can live courageously, knowing that you possess the ultimate protection: God's unfailing love for you.

The Rock of Ages is the great sheltering encirclement.

Oswald Chambers

Under heaven's lock and key, we are protected by the most efficient security system available: the power of God.

Charles Swindoll

A mighty fortress is our God, a bulwark never failing. Our helper He, amid the flood of mortal ills prevailing. For still our ancient foe doth seek to work us woe. His craft and power are great, armed with cruel hate, our earth is not his equal.

Martin Luther

As sure as God puts his children in the furnace, he will be in the furnace with them.

C. H. Spurgeon

A PRAYER FOR DADS

Lord, sometimes life is difficult. Sometimes, I am worried, weary, or heartbroken. And sometimes, I encounter powerful temptations to disobey Your commandments. But, when I lift my eyes to You, Father, You strengthen me. When I am weak, You lift me up. Today, I will turn to You for strength, for hope, for direction, and for deliverance. Amen

?QUESTION 74

It's hard for me to believe in miracles. What assurances can I find in the Bible?

THE QUICK ANSWER

If you're looking for miracles . . . you'll find them. If you're not, you won't.

Do You Believe in Miracles?

You are the God who performs miracles;
you display your power among the peoples.

Psalm 77:14 NIV

Do you believe that God is at work in the world? And do you also believe that nothing is impossible for Him? If so, then you also believe that God is perfectly capable of doing things that you, as a mere human being with limited vision and limited understanding, would deem to be utterly impossible. And that's precisely what God does.

Since the moment that He created our universe out of nothingness, God has made a habit of doing miraculous things. And He still works miracles today. Expect Him to work miracles in your own life, and then be watchful. With God, absolutely nothing is impossible, including an amazing assortment of miracles that He stands ready, willing, and able to perform for you and yours.

Miracles are not contrary to nature but only contrary to what we know about nature.

St. Augustine

Only God can move mountains, but faith and prayer can move God.

E. M. Bounds

Too many Christians live below the miracle level.

Vance Havner

The impossible is exactly what God does.

Oswald Chambers

A PRAYER FOR DADS

Lord, for You, nothing is impossible. Let me trust in Your power to do the miraculous, and let me trust in Your willingness to work miracles in my life—and in my heart. Amen

What does the Bible say about listening to God?

THE QUICK ANSWER

Prayer is two-way communication with God. Talking to God isn't enough; you should also listen to Him. If you and your family members want to gain a more intimate relationship with God, you should study His Word (every day), worship Him (every day), and talk to Him (many times every day). Remember: The more often you speak to the Creator, the more often He'll speak to you.

Listen Carefully

The one who is from God listens to God's words.
This is why you don't listen, because you are not from God.
John 8:47 Holman CSB

Sometimes God speaks loudly and clearly. More often, He speaks in a quiet voice—and if you are wise, you will be listening carefully when He does. To do so, you must carve out quiet moments each day to study His Word and sense His direction.

Can you quiet yourself long enough to listen to your conscience? Are you attuned to the subtle guidance of your intuition? Are you willing to pray sincerely and then to wait quietly for God's response? Hopefully so. Usually God refrains from sending His messages on stone tablets or city billboards. More often, He communicates in subtler ways. If you sincerely desire to hear His voice, you must listen carefully, and you must do so in the silent corners of your quiet, willing heart.

In the soul-searching of our lives, we are to stay quiet so we can hear Him say all that He wants to say to us in our hearts.

Charles Swindoll

We cannot experience the fullness of Christ if we do all the expressing. We must allow God to express His love, will, and truth to us.

Gary Smalley

When we come to Jesus stripped of pretensions, with a needy spirit, ready to listen, He meets us at the point of need.

Catherine Marshall

A PRAYER FOR DADS

Lord, give me the wisdom to be a good listener. Help me listen carefully to my family, to my friends, and—most importantly—to You. Amen

Sometimes the truth hurts. What does the Bible say about integrity?

THE QUICK ANSWER

The Bible leaves no room for doubt: Total honesty is the only path for those who seek to follow Christ. Truth sets you free; untruth imprisons you. So measure your words accordingly.

The Best Policy

Better to be poor and honest than a rich person no one can trust.
Proverbs 19:1 MSG

It has been said on many occasions and in many ways that honesty is the best policy. For believers, it is far more important to note that honesty is God's policy. And if we are to be servants worthy of Jesus Christ, we must be honest and forthright in our communications with others. Sometimes, honesty is difficult; sometimes, honesty is painful; sometimes, honesty is inconvenient; but always honesty is God's commandment.

In the Book of Proverbs, we read, "The Lord detests lying lips, but he delights in men who are truthful" (12:22 NIV). Clearly, we must strive to be men whose words are pleasing to our Creator. Truth is God's way, and it must be our way, too, even when telling the truth is difficult. As loving fathers, we can do no less.

Integrity is not a given factor in everyone's life. It is a result of self-discipline, inner trust, and a decision to be relentlessly honest in all situations in our lives.

John Maxwell

God doesn't expect you to be perfect, but he does insist on complete honesty.

Rick Warren

A little lie is like a little pregnancy. It doesn't take long before everyone knows.

C. S. Lewis

A PRAYER FOR DADS

Heavenly Father, You instruct Your children to seek truth and to live righteously. Help me always to live according to Your commandments. Sometimes, Lord, speaking the truth is difficult, but let me always speak truthfully and forthrightly. And, let me walk righteously and courageously so that others might see Your grace reflected in my words and my deeds. Amen

I've developed some bad habits. What should I do?

THE QUICK ANSWER

Target your most unhealthy habit first, and attack it with vigor. When it comes to defeating harmful habitual behaviors, you'll need focus, determination, prayer, more focus, more determination, and more prayer.

Healthy Habits

Do not be deceived: "Evil company corrupts good habits."
1 Corinthians 15:33 NKJV

It's an old saying and a true one: First, you make your habits, and then your habits make you. Some habits will inevitably bring you closer to God; other habits will lead you away from the path He has chosen for you. If you sincerely desire to improve your spiritual health, you must honestly examine the habits that make up the fabric of your day. And you must abandon those habits that are displeasing to God.

If you trust God, and if you keep asking for His help, He can transform your life. If you sincerely ask Him to help you, the same God who created the universe will help you defeat the harmful habits that have heretofore defeated you. So, if at first you don't succeed, keep praying. God is listening, and He's ready to help you become a better person if you ask Him . . . so ask today.

You will never change your life until you change something you do daily.

John Maxwell

The simple fact is that if we sow a lifestyle that is in direct disobedience to God's revealed Word, we ultimately reap disaster.

Charles Swindoll

Since behaviors become habits, make them work with you and not against you.

E. Stanley Jones

Prayer is a habit. Worship is a habit. Kindness is a habit. And if you want to please God, you'd better make sure that these habits are your habits.

Marie T. Freeman

A PRAYER FOR DADS

Dear Lord, help me break bad habits and form good ones. And let my actions be pleasing to You, today and every day. Amen

What does the Bible say about the need to share my personal testimony with family and friends?

THE QUICK ANSWER

If your eternity with God is secure (because you've given your heart to Jesus), you have a profound responsibility to tell as many people as you can about the eternal life that Christ offers to those who believe in Him. And, of course, it's up to you to make sure that your family members know where you stand.

Sharing Your Faith

But sanctify the Lord God in your hearts, and always be ready
to give a defense to everyone who asks you a reason
for the hope that is in you.
1 Peter 3:15 Holman CSB

Our personal testimonies are extremely important, but sometimes, because of shyness or insecurities, we're afraid to share our experiences. And that's unfortunate.

In his second letter to Timothy, Paul shares a message to believers of every generation when he writes, "God has not given us a spirit of timidity" (1:7). Paul's meaning is clear: When sharing our beliefs, we, as Christians, must be courageous, forthright, and unashamed.

We live in a world that desperately needs the healing message of Christ Jesus. Every believer, each in his or her own way, bears responsibility for sharing the Good News of our Savior.

Billy Graham observed, "Our faith grows by expression. If we want to keep our faith, we must share it." If you are a follower of Christ, the time to express your belief in Him is now. You know how He has touched your heart; help Him do the same for others.

Our Lord is searching for people who will make a difference. Christians dare not dissolve into the background or blend into the neutral scenery of the world.

Charles Swindoll

A PRAYER FOR DADS

Lord, the life that I live and the words that I speak will tell my family and the world how I feel about You. Today and every day, let my testimony be worthy of You. Let my words be sure and true, and let my actions point others to You. Amen

What does the Bible teach us about worship?

THE QUICK ANSWER

The best way for you and your family to worship God is to worship Him sincerely and often.

Family Worship

Worship the Lord with gladness. Come before him, singing with joy. Acknowledge that the Lord is God! He made us, and we are his. We are his people, the sheep of his pasture.
Psalm 100:2-3 NLT

When you lead your family in worship, you are to be praised. By worshipping your Creator—and by teaching your children to do likewise—you make a powerful statement about the place that God occupies in your life.

Ours is a society in which too many men have abandoned the moral leadership of their families, often with tragic consequences. Men who neglect to worship God, either thoughtlessly or intentionally, invite untold suffering into their own lives and into the lives of their loved ones.

Every day provides opportunities to put God where He belongs: at the center of our hearts. May we worship Him, and only Him, always. And, may we encourage the members of our family to do the same.

_____

Each of us needs a place of worship, such as our church. We need a place we can be reminded of God's Word and a place where we can revere His presence. Primarily, though, we worship in spirit, in the sanctuary of the heart.

Franklin Graham

When God is at the center of your life, you worship. When he's not, you worry.

Rick Warren

We worship God through service. The authentic server views each opportunity to lead or serve as an opportunity to worship God.

Bill Hybels

A PRAYER FOR DADS

Heavenly Father, let today and every day be a time of worship for me and my family. Let us worship You, not only with words, but also with deeds. In the quiet moments of the day, let us praise You and thank You for creating us, loving us, guiding us, and saving us. Amen

What does the Bible say about physical fitness?

THE QUICK ANSWER

God's Word teaches that your body is a miraculous gift from the Creator, and you should treat it that way.

Fitness Matters

Whatever you eat or drink or whatever you do,
you must do all for the glory of God.
1 Corinthians 10:31 NLT

Are you shaping up or spreading out? Do you eat sensibly and exercise regularly, or do you spend most of your time on the couch with a Twinkie in one hand and a clicker in the other? Are you choosing to treat your body like a temple or a trash heap? How you answer these questions will help determine how long you live and how well you live.

Physical fitness is a choice, a choice that requires discipline—it's as simple as that. So, do yourself this favor: treat your body like a one-of-a-kind gift from God . . . because that's precisely what your body is.

If you desire to improve your physical well-being and your emotional outlook, increasing your faith can help you.

John Maxwell

Jesus Christ is the One by Whom, for Whom, through Whom everything was made. Therefore, He knows what's wrong in your life and how to fix it.

Anne Graham Lotz

A Christian should no more defile his body than a Jew would defile the temple.

Warren Wiersbe

Our primary motivation should not be for more energy or to avoid a heart attack but to please God with our bodies.

Carole Lewis

A PRAYER FOR DADS

Dear Lord, my body is Your temple—I will treat it with care. Amen

At times, I feel discontented with life. How can I find lasting contentment?

THE QUICK ANSWER

Contentment comes, not from your circumstances, but from your attitude.

Genuine Contentment

I have learned to be content in whatever circumstances I am.
Philippians 4:11 Holman CSB

The preoccupation with happiness and contentment is an ever-present theme in the modern world. We are bombarded with messages that tell us where to find peace and pleasure in a world that worships materialism and wealth. But, lasting contentment is not found in material possessions; genuine contentment is a spiritual gift from God to those who trust in Him and follow His commandments.

Where can you and your family members find contentment? If you don't find it in God, you will never find it anywhere else. But, if you put your faith and your trust in Him, you will be blessed with an inner peace that is beyond human understanding. When God dwells at the center of your lives, peace and contentment will belong to you just as surely as you belong to God.

He is truly happy who has all that he wishes to have, and wishes to have nothing that he ought not to have.

St. Augustine

Contentment is difficult because nothing on earth can satisfy our deepest longing. We long to see God.

Max Lucado

Contentment is not escape from battle, but rather an abiding peace and confidence in the midst of battle.

Warren Wiersbe

Real contentment hinges on what's happening inside us, not around us.

Charles Stanley

A PRAYER FOR DADS

Dear Lord, let me strive to do Your will here on earth, and as I do, let me find contentment and balance. Let me live in the light of Your will and Your priorities for my life. And let me teach my children the peace and contentment that can be theirs through the gift of Your Son. Amen

When I displease God or injure other people, what can I do? How can I make things right with God?

THE QUICK ANSWER

If you're engaged in behavior that is displeasing to God, today is the day to stop. First, confess your sins to God. Then, ask Him what actions you should take in order to make things right again.

Real Repentance

The one who conceals his sins will not prosper,
but whoever confesses and renounces them will find mercy.
Proverbs 28:13 Holman CSB

Who among us has sinned? All of us. But, God calls upon us to turn away from sin by following His commandments. And the good news is this: When we do ask God's forgiveness and turn our hearts to Him, He forgives us absolutely and completely.

Genuine repentance requires more than simply offering God apologies for our misdeeds. Real repentance may start with feelings of sorrow and remorse, but it ends only when we turn away from the sin that has heretofore distanced us from our Creator. In truth, we offer our most meaningful apologies to God, not with our words, but with our actions. As long as we are still engaged in sin, we may be "repenting," but we have not fully "repented."

Is there an aspect of your life that is distancing you from your God? If so, ask for His forgiveness, and—just as importantly—stop sinning. Then, wrap yourself in the protection of God's Word. When you do, you will be secure.

But suppose we do sin. Suppose we slip and fall. Suppose we yield to temptation for a moment. What happens? We have to confess that sin.

Billy Graham

Repentance begins with confession of our guilt and recognition that our sin is against God.

Charles Stanley

A PRAYER FOR DADS

When I stray from Your commandments, Lord, I must not only confess my sins, I must also turn from them. When I fall short, help me to change. When I reject Your Word and Your will for my life, guide me back to Your side. Forgive my sins, Dear Lord, and help me live according to Your plan for my life. Your plan is perfect, Father; I am not. Let me trust in You. Amen

QUESTION 83

I'm a very busy father with a very full to-do list. What should I do?

THE QUICK ANSWER

Do first things first, and keep your focus on high-priority tasks. And remember this: your highest priority should be your relationship with God and His Son.

Too Busy?

Come to Me, all you who are weary and burdened,
and I will give you rest. Take My yoke upon you and learn from Me,
because I am gentle and humble in heart, and you will find rest for
your souls. For My yoke is easy and My burden is light.
Matthew 11:28-30 Holman CSB

Has the busy pace of life robbed you of the peace that might otherwise be yours through Jesus Christ? If so, you are simply too busy for your own good. Through His Son Jesus, God offers you a peace that passes human understanding, but He won't force His peace upon you; in order to experience it, you must slow down long enough to sense His presence and His love.

Today, as a gift to yourself, to your family, and to the world, slow down and claim the inner peace that is your spiritual birthright: the peace of Jesus Christ. It is offered freely; it has been paid for in full; it is yours for the asking. So ask. And then share.

———————————————

Busyness is the great enemy of relationships.

Rick Warren

Being busy, in and of itself, is not a sin. But being busy in an endless pursuit of things that leave us empty and hollow and broken inside—that cannot be pleasing to God.

Max Lucado

This is a day when we are so busy doing everything that we have no time to be anything. Even religiously we are so occupied with activities that we have no time to know God.

Vance Havner

A PRAYER FOR DADS

Dear Lord, sometimes, I am distracted by the busyness of the day or the demands of the moment. When I am worried or anxious, Father, turn my thoughts back to You. Help me to trust Your will, to follow Your commands, and to accept Your peace, today and forever. Amen

Sometimes I feel like my strength is almost gone. What can I do about that?

THE QUICK ANSWER

If you need strength, slow down, get more rest, engage in sensible exercise, and turn your troubles over to God . . . . but not necessarily in that order.

Need Strength?

Create in me a pure heart, O God, and renew a steadfast spirit within me. Do not cast me from your presence or take your Holy Spirit from me. Restore to me the joy of your salvation and grant me a willing spirit, to sustain me.
Psalm 51:10-12 NIV

God is a never-ending source of strength and courage if we call upon Him. When we are weary, He gives us strength. When we see no hope, God reminds us of His promises. When we grieve, God wipes away our tears.

Do you feel overwhelmed by today's responsibilities? Do you feel pressured by the ever-increasing demands of 21st-century life? Then turn your concerns and your prayers over to God. He knows your needs, and He has promised to meet those needs.

Whatever your circumstances, God will protect you and care for you . . . if you let Him. Invite Him into your heart and allow Him to renew your spirits. When you trust Him and Him alone, He will never fail you.

Walking with God leads to receiving his intimate counsel, and counseling leads to deep restoration.

John Eldredge

One reason so much American Christianity is a mile wide and an inch deep is that Christians are simply tired. Sometimes you need to kick back and rest for Jesus' sake.

Dennis Swanberg

The resurrection of Jesus Christ is the power of God to change history and to change lives.

Bill Bright

A PRAYER FOR DADS

Dear Lord, sometimes the demands of the day leave me discouraged and frustrated. Renew my strength, Father, and give me patience and perspective. Today and every day, let me draw comfort and courage from Your promises, from Your love, and from Your Son. Amen

What does God's Word say about grace?

THE QUICK ANSWER

God's grace is always available. Jim Cymbala writes, "No one is beyond his grace. No situation, anywhere on earth, it too hard for God." If you sincerely seek God's grace, He will give it freely. So ask, and you will receive.

The Ultimate Treasure: God's Grace

Grace to you and peace from God our Father
and the Lord Jesus Christ.
Philippians 1:2 NASB

Someone has said that GRACE stands for God's Redemption At Christ's Expense. It's true—God sent His Son so that we might be redeemed from our sins. In doing so, our Heavenly Father demonstrated His infinite mercy and His infinite love. We have received countless gifts from God, but none can compare with the gift of salvation. God's grace is the ultimate gift, and we owe Him the ultimate in thanksgiving.

The gift of eternal life is the priceless possession of everyone who accepts God's Son as Lord and Savior. We return our

Savior's love by welcoming Him into our hearts and sharing His message and His love. When we do so, we are blessed today and forever.

The grace of God is sufficient for all our needs, for every problem, and for every difficulty, for every broken heart, and for every human sorrow.

Peter Marshall

You don't earn grace, and you don't deserve grace; you simply receive it as God's loving gift, and then share it with others.

Warren Wiersbe

Grace is an outrageous blessing bestowed freely on a totally undeserving recipient.

Bill Hybels

A PRAYER FOR DADS

Lord, You have saved me by Your grace. Keep me mindful that Your grace is a gift that I can accept but cannot earn. I praise You for that priceless gift, today and forever. Let me share the good news of Your grace with a world that desperately needs Your healing touch. Amen

QUESTION 86

What does the Bible say about righteousness?

THE QUICK ANSWER

Because God is just, He rewards righteousness just as surely as He punishes sin. Try as we might, we simply cannot escape the consequences of our actions. How we behave today has a direct impact on the rewards we will receive tomorrow. That's a lesson that we must teach our children by our words and our actions, but not necessarily in that order.

Doing the Right Thing

Lead a tranquil and quiet life in all godliness and dignity.
1 Timothy 2:2 Holman CSB

Oswald Chambers, the author of the Christian classic *My Utmost For His Highest*, advised, "Never support an experience which does not have God as its source, and faith in God as its result." These words serve as a powerful reminder that, as Christians, we are called to walk with God and obey His commandments. But, we live in a world that presents countless temptations for adults and even more temptations for our children.

We Christians, when confronted with sin, have clear instructions: walk—or better yet run—in the opposite direction.

When we do, we reap the blessings that God has promised to all those who live according to His will and His Word.

The best evidence of our having the truth is our walking in the truth.

Matthew Henry

If we have the true love of God in our hearts, we will show it in our lives. We will not have to go up and down the earth proclaiming it. We will show it in everything we say or do.

D. L. Moody

We must appropriate the tender mercy of God every day after conversion, or problems quickly develop. We need his grace daily in order to live a righteous life.

Jim Cymbala

A PRAYER FOR DADS

Holy Father, let my thoughts and my deeds be pleasing to You. I thank You, Lord, for Jesus, the One who took away my sins. Today and every day, I will follow in His footsteps so that my life can be a living testimony to Your love, to Your forgiveness, and to Your Son. Amen

Sometimes I'm worried about the future. What does God's Word say about my future?

THE QUICK ANSWER

If you've given your heart to Jesus, God's Word promises that your future is intensely bright. Of course, you and your loved ones may encounter adversity and pain, but your eternal destiny is secure.

Your Bright Future

What a God we have! And how fortunate we are to have him, this Father of our Master Jesus! Because Jesus was raised from the dead, we've been given a brand-new life and have everything to live for, including a future in heaven—and the future starts now!
1 Peter 1:3-4 MSG

How bright is your future? Well, if you're a faithful believer, God's plans for you are so bright that you'd better wear shades. But here's an important question: How bright do you believe your future to be? Are you expecting a terrific tomorrow, or are you dreading a terrible one? The answer you give will have a powerful impact on the way tomorrow turns out.

Do you trust in the ultimate goodness of God's plan for your life? Will you face tomorrow's challenges with optimism and hope? You should. After all, God created you for a very important reason: His reason. And you still have important work to do: His work.

Today, as you live in the present and look to the future, remember that God has an amazing plan for you. Act—and believe—accordingly.

Hoping for a good future without investing in today is like a farmer waiting for a crop without ever planting any seed.

John Maxwell

The pages of your past cannot be rewritten, but the pages of your tomorrows are blank.

Zig Ziglar

Joy comes from knowing God loves me and knows who I am and where I'm going . . . that my future is secure as I rest in Him.

James Dobson

A PRAYER FOR DADS

Dear Lord, as I look to the future, I will place my trust in You. If I become discouraged, I will turn to You. If I am afraid, I will seek strength in You. You are my Father, and I will place my hope, my trust, and my faith in You. Amen

What does the Bible say about sin?

THE QUICK ANSWER

Every day of your life, you will be tempted to sin, to rebel against God's teachings. Your job, simply put, is to guard your heart against the darkness as you focus on the light.

Ignoring Sin

For everyone who practices wicked things hates the light
and avoids it, so that his deeds may not be exposed.
But anyone who lives by the truth comes to the light,
so that his works may be shown to be accomplished by God.
John 3:20–21 Holman CSB

If we deny our sins, we allow those sins to flourish. And if we allow sinful behaviors to become habits, we invite hardships into our own lives and into the lives of our loved ones. When we yield to the distractions and temptations of this troubled world, we suffer. But God has other intentions, and His plans for our lives do not include sin or denial.

When we allow ourselves to encounter God's presence, He will lead us away from temptation, away from confusion, and away from the self-deception. God is the champion of truth and the enemy of denial. May we see ourselves through His eyes and conduct ourselves accordingly.

What I like about experience is that it is such an honest thing. You may take any number of wrong turnings; but keep your eyes open and you will not be allowed to go very far before the warning signs appear. You may have deceived yourself, but experience is not trying to deceive you. The universe rings true wherever you fairly test it.

C. S. Lewis

Any act gains in power as it moves inward toward the heart. For this reason, the sins of the spirit are more iniquitous than those of the body.

A. W. Tozer

A PRAYER FOR DADS

Dear Lord, when I displease You, I do injury to myself, to my family, and to my community. Because sin distances me from You, Lord, I will fear sin and I will avoid sinful places. The fear of sinning against You is a healthy fear, Father, because it can motivate me to accomplish Your will. Let a healthy fear of sin guide my path, today and every day of my life. Amen

? QUESTION 89

Some people are hard to get along with. How should I deal with difficult people?

THE QUICK ANSWER

Forgiveness should not be confused with enabling. Even after you've forgiven the difficult person in your life, you are not compelled to accept continued mistreatment from him or her.

Dealing with Difficult People

Hatred stirs up trouble, but love forgives all wrongs.
Proverbs 10:12 NCV

Sometimes, people can be discourteous and cruel. Sometimes people can be unfair, unkind, and unappreciative. Sometimes people get angry and frustrated. So what's a Christian to do? God's answer is straightforward: forgive, forget, and move on. In Luke 6:37, Jesus instructs, "Do not judge, and you will not be judged. Do not condemn, and you will not be condemned. Forgive, and you will be forgiven" (Holman CSB).

Today and every day, make sure that you're quick to

forgive others for their shortcomings. And when other people misbehave (as they most certainly will from time to time), don't pay too much attention. Just forgive those people as quickly as you can, and try to move on . . . as quickly as you can.

Sour godliness is the devil's religion.

John Wesley

One way or the other, God, who thought up the family in the first place, has the very best idea of how to bring sense to the chaos of broken relationships we see all around us. I really believe that if I remain still and listen a lot, He will share some solutions with me so I can share them with others.

Jill Briscoe

Some folks cause happiness wherever they go, others whenever they go.

Barbara Johnson

A PRAYER FOR DADS

Dear Lord, sometimes people can be difficult to live with. Just as I want forgiveness from others, help me forgive those who have caused me inconvenience or pain. And let the love of Your Son fill my heart so that there is no room for bitterness, anger, or regret. Amen

I can be very hard on myself at times. What does the Bible say about my self-worth?

THE QUICK ANSWER

Don't worry too much about self-worth: Instead, worry more about living a life that is pleasing to God. Learn to think optimistically. Find a worthy purpose. Find people to love and people to serve. When you do, your self-worth will, on most days, take care of itself.

Your Own Worst Critic?

Those who wait for perfect weather will never plant seeds;
those who look at every cloud will never harvest crops . . . .
Plant early in the morning, and work until evening, because you
don't know if this or that will succeed. They might both do well.
Ecclesiastes 11:4, 6 NCV

When God made you, He equipped you with an array of talents and abilities that are uniquely yours. It's up to you to discover those talents and to use them, but sometimes your own perfectionism may get in the way.

If you're your own worst critic, give it up. After all, God doesn't expect you to be perfect, and if that's okay with Him, then it should be okay with you, too.

When you accepted Christ as your Savior, God accepted you for all eternity. Now, it's your turn to accept yourself. When you do, you'll feel a tremendous weight being lifted from your shoulders. And that's as it should be. After all, only one earthly being ever lived life to perfection, and He was the Son of God. The rest of us have fallen short of God's standard and need to be accepting of our own limitations as well as the limitations of others.

The happiest people in the world are not those who have no problems, but the people who have learned to live with those things that are less than perfect.

James Dobson

What makes a Christian a Christian is not perfection but forgiveness.

Max Lucado

A PRAYER FOR DADS

Lord, this world has so many expectations of me, but today I will not seek to meet the world's expectations; I will do my best to meet Your expectations. I will make You my ultimate priority, Lord, by serving You, by praising You, by loving You, and by obeying You. Amen

What does the Bible say about God's plans for my family and for me?

THE QUICK ANSWER

God has a wonderful plan for you and your loved ones. And the time to start looking for that plan—and living it—is now. Discovering God's plan begins with prayer, but it doesn't end there. You've also got to work at it.

Big Plans

"I say this because I know what I am planning for you,"
says the Lord. "I have good plans for you, not plans to hurt you.
I will give you hope and a good future."
Jeremiah 29:11 NCV

The Bible makes it clear: God has plans—very big plans—for you and your family. But He won't force His plans upon you—if you wish to experience the abundance that God has in store, you must be willing to accept His will and follow His Son.

As Christians, you and your family members should ask yourselves this question: "How closely can we make our plans match God's plans?" The more closely you manage to follow the path that God intends for your lives, the better.

99 QUESTIONS—GOD'S ANSWERS FOR DADS

Do you and your loved ones have questions or concerns about the future? Take them to God in prayer. Do you have hopes and expectations? Talk to God about your dreams. Are you and your family members carefully planning for the days and weeks ahead? Consult God as you establish your priorities. Turn every concern over to your Heavenly Father, and sincerely seek His guidance—prayerfully, earnestly, and often. Then, listen for His answers . . . and trust the answers that He gives.

The Almighty does nothing without reason, although the frail mind of man cannot explain the reason.

St. Augustine

The Christian life is one of faith, where we find ourselves routinely overdriving our headlights but knowing it's okay because God is in control and has a purpose behind it.

Bill Hybels

A PRAYER FOR DADS

Dear Lord, I will seek Your plan for my life. Even when I don't understand why things happen, I will trust You. Even when I am uncertain of my next step, I will trust You. There are many things that I cannot do, Lord, and there are many things that I cannot understand. But one thing I can do is to trust You always. And I will. Amen

? QUESTION 92

Sometimes, life seems so serious. What should our family do about it?

THE QUICK ANSWER

God's Word instructs us to be joyful. As a parent, it's up to you to make certain that your house is a place where everybody can expect to have good clean fun and plenty of laughs.

So Laugh!

Laugh with your happy friends when they're happy;
share tears when they're down.
Romans 12:15 MSG

Laughter is a gift from God, a gift that He intends for us to use. Yet sometimes, because of the inevitable stresses of everyday living, we fail to find the fun in life. When we allow life's inevitable disappointments to cast a pall over our lives and our souls, we do a profound disservice to ourselves and to our loved ones.

If you've allowed the clouds of life to obscure the blessings of life, perhaps you've formed the unfortunate habit of taking things just a little too seriously. If so, it's time to fret a little less and laugh a little more.

So today, look for the humor that most certainly surrounds you—when you do, you'll find it. And remember: God created laughter for a reason . . . and Father indeed knows best. So laugh!

Laughter is like premium gasoline: It takes the knock out of living.

Anonymous

I think everybody ought to be a laughing Christian. I'm convinced that there's just one place where there's not any laughter, and that's hell.

Jerry Clower

If you want people to feel comfortable around you, to enjoy being with you, then learn to laugh at yourself and find humor in life's little mishaps.

Dennis Swanberg

A PRAYER FOR DADS

Lord, when I begin to take myself or my life too seriously, let me laugh. When I rush from place to place, slow me down, Lord, and let me laugh. Put a smile on my face, Dear Lord, and let me share that smile with all who cross my path . . . and let me laugh. Amen

?QUESTION 93

It's hard not to be judgmental of other people, and it's hard not to judge their motives. What does the Bible say about judging others?

THE QUICK ANSWER

Your ability to judge others requires a divine insight that you simply don't have. So do everybody (including yourself) a favor: don't judge.

Let God Judge

Stop judging others, and you will not be judged.
Stop criticizing others, or it will all come back on you.
If you forgive others, you will be forgiven.
Luke 6:37 NLT

We have all fallen short of God's commandments, and He has forgiven us. We, too, must forgive others. And, we must refrain from judging them.

Are you one of those people who finds it easy to judge others? If so, it's time to change.

God does not need (or, for that matter, want) your help. Why? Because God is perfectly capable of judging the human heart . . . while you are not.

As Christians, we are warned that to judge others is to invite fearful consequences: to the extent we judge others, so, too, will we be judged by God. Let us refrain, then, from judging our neighbors. Instead, let us forgive them and love them in the same way that God has forgiven us.

Being critical of others, including God, is one way we try to avoid facing and judging our own sins.

Warren Wiersbe

Don't judge other people more harshly than you want God to judge you.

Marie T. Freeman

Christians think they are prosecuting attorneys or judges, when, in reality, God has called all of us to be witnesses.

Warren Wiersbe

A PRAYER FOR DADS

Dear Lord, sometimes I am quick to judge others. But, You have commanded me not to judge. Keep me mindful, Father, that when I judge others, I am living outside of Your will for my life. You have forgiven me, Lord. Let me forgive others, let me love them, and let me help them . . . without judging them. Amen

Sometimes, it's easy to think, "I've done that," when it was, in truth, God who did it. So what does the Bible say about humility?

THE QUICK ANSWER

God favors the humble just as surely as He disciplines the proud. So you must remain humble or face the consequences. Pride does go before the fall, but humility often prevents the fall.

The Wisdom to Be Humble

God has chosen you and made you his holy people. He loves you.
So always do these things: Show mercy to others,
be kind, humble, gentle, and patient.
Colossians 3:12 NCV

Hopefully, you are a proud papa. God intends that you take appropriate parental pride in every member of your family. But God has a stern warning for those who would take undue pride in their own accomplishments. Excessive pride is a sin.

As Christians, we have a profound reason to be humble: We have been refashioned and saved by Jesus Christ, and that salvation came not because of our own good works but because of God's grace. Thus, we are not "self-made"; we are "God-made" and "Christ-saved." How, then, can we be boastful? The answer, of course, is simple: if we are to be honest with ourselves and with our God, we cannot be boastful. In the quiet moments, when we search the depths of our own hearts, we know that whatever "it" is, God did that. And He deserves the credit.

God exalts humility. When God works in our lives, helping us to become humble, he gives us a permanent joy. Humility gives us a joy that cannot be taken away.

Max Lucado

It was pride that changed angels into devils; it is humility that makes men as angels.

St. Augustine

A PRAYER FOR DADS

Heavenly Father, Jesus clothed Himself with humility when He chose to leave heaven and come to earth to live and die for us, His children. Christ is my Master and my example. Clothe me with humility, Lord, so that I might be more like Your Son, and keep me mindful that You are the giver and sustainer of life, and to You, Dear Lord, goes the glory and the praise. Amen

Sometimes, I become discouraged, and sometimes I'm worried. What should I do?

THE QUICK ANSWER

If you believe the promises contained in God's Word, your future—and your family's future—is secure. So when you consider God's blessings, you should be thankful, optimistic, and ready to serve.

Watching the Donut

I can do everything through him that gives me strength.
Philippians 4:13 NIV

On the wall of a little donut shop, the sign said: As you travel through life, brother, whatever be your goal, keep your eye upon the donut, and not upon the hole.

Are you a Christian who keeps your eye upon the donut, or have you acquired the bad habit of looking only at the hole? Hopefully, you spend most of your waking hours looking at the donut (and thanking God for it).

Christianity and pessimism don't mix. So do yourself a favor: choose to be a hope-filled Christian. Think optimistically about your life and your future. Trust your hopes, not your fears. Take time to celebrate God's glorious creation. And then, when you've filled your heart with hope and gladness, share your optimism with your friends. They'll be better for it, and so will you. But not necessarily in that order.

The people whom I have seen succeed best in life have always been cheerful and hopeful people who went about their business with a smile on their faces.

Charles Kingsley

Do you feel the world is treating you well? If your attitude toward the world is excellent, you will receive excellent results. If you feel so-so about the world, your response from that world will be average. If you feel badly about your world, you will seem to have only negative feedback from life.

John Maxwell

A PRAYER FOR DADS

Lord, let me be an expectant Christian. Let me expect the best from You, and let me look for the best in others. If I become discouraged, Father, turn my thoughts and my prayers to You. Let me trust You, Lord, to direct my life. And, let me share my faith and optimism with others, today and every day that I live. Amen

QUESTION 96

This world can be a crazy place for grownups and kids alike. What should I do about the evils that I encounter? And what about the temptations my children will encounter?

THE QUICK ANSWER

Of course there is darkness in this world, but God's light can overpower any darkness. So make sure that your family's life—and faith—is built on the firm foundation of God's Word. Make sure that your children have plenty of "advance warning" (from you) about the dangers they will encounter. And keep praying that everyone in your clan will have the wisdom and the strength to avoid the darkness.

On Guard Against Evil

Your love must be real. Hate what is evil,
and hold on to what is good.
Romans 12:9 NCV

Nineteenth-century clergyman Edwin Hubbel Chapin warned, "Neutral men are the devil's allies." His words were true then, and they're true now. Neutrality in the face of evil is a sin. Yet all too often, we fail to fight evil, not because we are neutral, but because we are shortsighted: we don't fight the devil because we don't recognize his handiwork.

If we are to recognize evil and fight it, we must pay careful attention. We must pay attention to God's Word, and we must pay attention to the realities of everyday life. When we observe life objectively, and when we do so with eyes and hearts that are attuned to God's Holy Word, we can no longer be neutral believers. And when we are no longer neutral, God rejoices while the devil despairs.

God loves you, and He yearns for you to turn away from the path of evil. You need His forgiveness, and you need Him to come into your life and remake you from within.

Billy Graham

God shapes the world by prayer. The more praying there is in the world, the better the world will be, and the mightier will be the forces against evil.

E. M. Bounds

A PRAYER FOR DADS

Lord, strengthen my walk with You. Evil comes in many disguises, and sometimes it is only with Your help that I can recognize right from wrong. Your presence in my life enables me to choose truth and to live a life pleasing to You. May I always live in Your presence. Amen

Sometimes I have doubts about my future and doubts about my faith. What should I do?

THE QUICK ANSWER

When you have doubts, it is important to take those doubts to the Lord.

When You Have Doubts

An indecisive man is unstable in all his ways.

James 1:8 Holman CSB

If you're a dad who's never had any doubts about his faith, you can stop reading this page now and skip to the next. But if you've ever been plagued by doubts about your faith or your God, keep reading.

Even some of the most faithful Christians are, at times, beset by occasional bouts of discouragement and doubt. But even when we feel far removed from God, God is never far removed from us. He is always with us, always willing to calm the storms of life—always willing to replace our doubts with comfort and assurance.

Whenever you're plagued by doubts, that's precisely the moment you should seek God's presence by genuinely seeking to establish a deeper, more meaningful relationship with His Son. Then you may rest assured that in time, God will calm your fears, answer your prayers, and restore your confidence.

Doubt may not always be a sign that a man is wrong; it may be a sign that he is thinking.

Oswald Chambers

We basically have two choices to make in dealing with the mysteries of God. We can wrestle with Him or we can rest in Him.

Calvin Miller

Mark it down. God never turns away the honest seeker. Go to God with your questions. You may not find all the answers, but in finding God, you know the One who does.

Max Lucado

A PRAYER FOR DADS

Dear God, sometimes this world can be a puzzling place, filled with uncertainty and doubt. When I am unsure of my next step, keep me mindful that You are always near and that You can overcome any challenge. Give me faith, Father, and let me remember always that with Your love and Your power, I can live courageously and faithfully today and every day. Amen

How does God want me to love my family?

THE QUICK ANSWER

Parental love should be demonstrated with deeds, not just announced with words. You demonstrate your love by giving of yourself and your time. While you're with your child, be sure to watch carefully and listen with your ears, your eyes, and your heart. And remember: wise parents pay careful attention to the things their children don't say.

A Father's Love

This is my command: Love one another the way I loved you.
This is the very best way to love.
Put your life on the line for your friends.
John 15:12-13 MSG

Few things in life can compare with a father's love or a father's smile. And because God has blessed us more richly than we could ever deserve, we fathers have many reasons to flash our pearly whites. But being a responsible dad in a demanding world is not always a cause for boundless celebration. Sometimes, being a fully involved parent is tough work.

Parenting is a full-time job; it is a lifetime commitment with great responsibilities and the potential for even greater rewards. Our challenge, as parents, is to raise our children lovingly, responsibly, and according to God's commandments. When we do, the difficult job of parenting is made easier, and our families are forever blessed.

Christian love, either towards God or towards man, is an affair of the will.

C. S. Lewis

Homes that are built on anything other than love are bound to crumble.

Billy Graham

The truth of the Gospel is intended to free us to love God and others with our whole heart.

John Eldredge

A PRAYER FOR DADS

Lord, You have given me the gift of love and You've asked me to share it. The gift of love is a precious gift indeed. Let me nurture love and treasure it. And, help me remember that the essence of love is not to receive it, but to give it, today and forever. Amen

QUESTION 99

What promises does God's Word make about salvation?

THE QUICK ANSWER

God offers you life abundant and life eternal. Accept God's salvation through Jesus Christ and begin to live.

For God So Loved the World

This is how much God loved the world: He gave his Son, his one and only Son. And this is why: so that no one need be destroyed; by believing in him anyone can have a whole and lasting life.

John 3:16 MSG

Christ sacrificed His life on the cross so that we might have eternal life. This gift, freely given by God's only begotten Son, is the priceless possession of everyone who accepts Him as Lord and Savior. God is waiting patiently for each of us to accept the gift of eternal life. Let us claim Christ's gift today.

It is by God's grace that we have been saved, through faith. We are saved not because of our good deeds but because of our faith in Christ. May we, who have been given so much, praise our Savior for the gift of salvation, and may we share the joyous news of our Master's love and His grace.

God did everything necessary to provide for our forgiveness by sacrificing His perfect, holy Son as the atoning substitute for our sins.

Franklin Graham

The way to be saved is not to delay, but to come and take.

D. L. Moody

The essence of salvation is an about-face from self-centeredness to God-centeredness.

Henry Blackaby

There is no detour to holiness. Jesus came to the resurrection through the cross, not around it.

Leighton Ford

A PRAYER FOR DADS

Dear Lord, I am only here on this earth for a brief while. But, You have offered me the priceless gift of eternal life through Your Son Jesus. I accept Your gift, Lord, with thanksgiving and praise. Let me share the Good News of my salvation with all those who need Your healing touch. Amen